Cast Away

For these reasons

Economic Jihad

Jo M. Sekimonyo

Venus flytrap Press

Cambridge Boston New York

venusflytrappress@gmail.com
Venus flytrap Press, LLC
P.O. Box 390780
Cambridge, MA 02139

Venus Flytrap Press can bring the author to your live event.

Editing and interior design by Tara Casimir
Jacket Photographs: http://www.123rf.com

All quotations remain the intellectual property of their respective originators. All use of quotations is done under the fair use copyright principal.

Includes bibliographical references and index.

1.   Ethosism   2. Political Economy   3. Capitalism-Barbarism
       4. Abstinence Theory   5. Common sense I. Title.

Library of Congress Control Number: 2014953123

ISBN: 978-0-9908674-0-1 (Hardcover)
ISBN: 978-0-9908674-1-8 (Paperback)
ISBN: 978-0-9908674-2-5 (Kindle)
ISBN: 978-0-9908674-3-2 (Nook)
ISBN: 978-0-9908674-4-9 (iBook)

Content

LETTER TO MAMA VINCENT   I

ACKNOWLEDGMENTS V

INTERLUDE I   1

I   INTRODUCTION   3

II   KAMIKAZE 13

III I SEE POOR PEOPLE 23

INTERLUDE II 43

IV   GANGNAM STYLE 45

V   FALSE PROPHESIES   63

VI   CORRUPTIBILIS   83

INTERLUDE III 93

VII MOHAMED BOUAZIZI   95

VIII SAY WHAAAT?!! 111

INTERLUDE IV 133

IX   D.R.I.P. 135

X   DIAMONDS ARE A WOMAN'S BFF 141

XI   HOP-O'-MY-THUMB   155

INTERLUDE V 169

XII CURRENT AND RUDE STATE OF SOCIETY   171

XIII ABRACADABRA   187

SKY HIGH   211

FULL CIRCLE   217

NOTES 221

INDEX 231

SPECIAL THANKS   243

AND FINALLY 247

Letter to Mama Vincent

"There is a common tendency to ignore the poor or to develop some rationalization for the good fortune of the fortunate."

John Kenneth Galbraith

Dear Mama Vincent,

If this letter comes as a surprise to you, then you have no idea of the profound impression that our encounter with you has had in our life since that day. Putting faces to the global malaise has kept my wife and myself from sailing conscience free around the ocean of the abstract. I sincerely commend you for taking full responsibility of the bad decisions you have made in your life, but I would be foolish to believe that your slip-ups are all there is to the story. In reality, from your birth, the odds were already stacked against you, and I know how this part of the world is merciless to single illiterate mothers. Vincent could have easily been me if I had landed in my mother's hands.

Dear, under your beautiful smile and joyful laugh, I saw an excruciating pain. You still have your life ahead of you. You shouldn't be a nameless figure, giving up on your big dreams and aspirations just yet. Then again, holding Vincent in my arms, under roaming eyes of law enforcement agents passing by, I for a moment shared your agony and despair.

It is touching the way you come to describe your son Vincent as your reason to live. Most of the young people your age use such poignant statements to refer to the cute boy or girl they come to believe are their soul mates, the same person they will eventually dump for some blasé reason with little if any remorse. Even worse, it is revolting to overhear grownups reduce life's meaning into ephemeral passing of emotions. Still, I cannot ignore that your reality in Kenya is far different than people in my current world.

You confessed to us that at times, you feel hopeless, a pariah creeping through the streets in the vibrant city of Nairobi, which has decided to criminalize poverty. It is not a surprise that Nairobi's zero tolerance on the depraved has created the largest landfill of the poor in the whole Eastern region of Africa, the slum of Kibera. Yet it breaks my heart to say there are other Kiberas and worse around this suffocating blue planet which is not comforting to you either. From my travels, I have seen countless young mothers with their children panhandling all over the Democratic Republic of Congo and on every corner in Addis Ababa Ethiopia, and men in faded uniforms begging for coins on main streets in crumbling cities across the United States of America.

I have been on an investigative journey dissecting the hardships endured by Brazilians living in the City of God, the inhabitants of Cite' Jalousie in Port-au-Prince, Haiti before and after the devastating earthquake, the Romanians in Blagoevgrad Bulgaria, Russians clustered in the Ghetto of Tver City, and the poor in Kowloon Walled City, Hong Kong, China. I have been surprised by the residents' resilience of crime and poverty infected cities such as Detroit US and San Salvador capital of El Salvador. And it is sad to say around the world there are billions of people just like you who will go their whole lives experiencing poverty, famine, homelessness, and abuse that will most likely occur in the hands of law enforcement agents.

Tara and I are well aware that the few Kenyan shilling bills we gave you equated to scarce meals and a shelter for only a couple of days. After what you and Vincent probably had to do to survive, is getting back on Nairobi's mean streets, at the mercy of other compassionate souls. We are deeply sorry that we couldn't rescue you and others from this nightmare.

After walking by, giving my spare change to people blinded and asphyxiated by misery, I asked myself repeatedly, what else can I do?! Stories about inequality have been told on and on. Nevertheless, I decided to stir the debate onto a new path that could give Vincent, and other innocent children like him, a chance to a decent life. My mantra is Vincent should have not just a roof over his head but a home, not just water but clean drinks, not just food but healthy meals, not just a classroom but quality education. And all these factors should eventually lead him to not just a job but at least a universal living recompense for his skills and abilities. Anything less would be regarded as humanity's failure and continuing tragedy!!!

Sincerely,

Jo M. Sekimonyo

Acknowledgments

"If you want to change the world, pick up your pen and write."

Martin Luther

Tara and I met in Tampa Florida; she had embarked on a great career that required long hours on her feet but provided the financial security that her parents, Haitian immigrants, have dreamed of. In contrast, I was a hippy lunatic idealist which my pap found outlandish. Somehow, I was able to convince her to parachute out of her stable and bright quotidian life to join me into the dark side. What really got into her head to gamble on me and on graduate school prospects? As diabolic speculations gained traction, we relocated to the north-eastern part of United States; what a relief.

Our first snow was interesting for me, to say the least. It was the first time Tara gave me the "serial killer look", holding a sharp knife, and didn't say a word for a minute. Bear in mind that even in my sleep, I would throw a tantrum denouncing the increasing gap between the "have a lot" and the "have squat" all over the globe. Little that I knew, my lovely wife was fed up of my homilies and wailings of the global socio-economic malaise, and more-so of my plans to present to the world what I believe is the remedy. Sure, I jotted down notes on gazillions of papers that laid like dead leaves on our office floor, but stopping short of mustering the energy and discipline to complete a manuscript. A family friend even suggested that I put my ideas into a book so that I can amass followers; build a cult? A preposterous idea, at the time. As much as it pains me to admit it, Tara was right. I had talked the talk for years, it was time that I walked the walk, or in this case, wrote the write.

Why is the title of this book not 'Economics Codex Gigas'? Well, Nassau Senior beat me to writing the economic devil's bible. Cast Away? Economic Jihad? Your slothful mind could be rushing to a certain conclusion right now. Chill pills will be handy on this journey; this book excavates long standing challenges that generations of indolent economists and their groupies have suppressed or pointed in the wrong direction for two centuries. This is neither clandestine parody nor a callous demonstration of prowess, but a genuine and provocative dissection of our world and the economic discipline.

Other than my anger and anxiety, I have to thank people that happen to sit next to me in greyhound buses during my frequent exhausting commutes and with whom I had some of the most memorable discussions of my existence. Among them, a head of a University who had really harsh words for the Nobel Prize economist, Milton Friedman for coming from a humble Jewish family beginning in New York city and "turning into an asshole" (his words). Also to my special sauce of ingredients, friends and foes who have been driven by the insatiable appetite of proving my ideas were crazy;

you have helped me strengthen my arguments and conviction, I love you, ladies and gentlemen.

Most of all, I am more than thankful for my wife, my partner in crime, for her excessive but effective tactics instrumental for me to undertake the daunting task of writing this book.

The relevance of Heterox economics is more than ever before threatened. Already, a number of Heterox economic programs have been disbanded. If the institutions that are immersed in this school of economic thought stay on the same track and don't adjust their goal from producing economists who aspire to become successful theoreticians, thinkers, to whom are going to become accomplished pragmatists, reasoning humans, their role in this global competitive academia will become obsolete. The end of heterox economics might also be the best thing for the revival of institutionalism or even better, institutions adoption and dissemination of *Ethosism*, a more lucid and relevant moral stream.

Interlude I

"Our deepest fear is not that we are inadequate. Our deepest fear is that we are powerful beyond measure. It is our light, not our darkness that most frightens us. We ask ourselves, who am I to be brilliant, gorgeous, talented, and fabulous? Actually, who are you not to be? You are a child of God. Your playing small does not serve the world. There is nothing enlightened about shrinking so that other people won't feel insecure around you. We are all meant to shine, as children do. We were born to make manifest the glory of God that is within us. It's not just in some of us; it's in everyone. And as we let our own light shine, we unconsciously give other people permission to do the same. As we are liberated from our own fear, our presence automatically liberates others."

This inspiring quote by Marianne Williamson is from her book, A Return to Love: *Reflections on the Principles of a Course in Miracles*, Harper Collins, 1992. From Chapter 7, Section 3 (Pg. 190-191). Even though Nelson Mandela never uttered this quote in his 1994 inaugural speech, for my generation, it is forever attached with the man. If something has to be objectively said about his one term as the President of South Africa, his cowardly rainbow approach on dissolving apartheid had made him the white South African bourgeois champion. And, of course, if one simply tries to look at him within the context of a man who spent twenty seven years in prison without begging his masters for a pardon or cracking the skull of another inmate, he has in essence, deserved to be held as one of the mythical figures of the power of conviction who exemplifies the strength of character required in the struggle against socio-economic inequality. What other better way to limp into the next phase of this expedition?

Introduction

"Art is an attempt to integrate evil."
                    Simone de Beauvoir

I don't listen to compact discs. I play old tunes on vinyl. Perusing through thrift stores in search of a Sam Cooke, a Wendo Kolosoy, a Thelonious Monk, an Eduardo Sanchez de Fuentes, a Jimmie Rodgers, a Notorious B.I.G, a Mikhail Glinka, a Mariam Makeba, a Nana Mouskouri, a Fela Kuti, a Claude Debussy, or a Sergei Sergeyevich Prokofiev is as soothing as yoga. I treasure authentic Peruvian folklore music beats and Mongolian musical instruments more than a pop artist funk or tarnished and unusual twisted spoons' exhibition. For me, any form of expression that ceases to be an experience and becomes an art form loses its glowing divinity. In the same spirit, this book is an experience, not an artistic acrobatic exercise meant for viewing to remind you that it exists.

I have been excommunicated from a long list of tea shops and bars on the bogus charge of being a Marxist sorcerer or Ferdinand Lassalle embodiment. The general public wrongly ties together an economic status quo examination with anti-Capitalism bravura based on an acute paranoia of the Karl Marx book 'Das Kapital'. If you don't believe me, try to turn the light on

the ugliest Capitalism facets, and bam, you get
ostracized from the society as a Communist. Yet
prompting a conversation on a new robust alternative to
Capitalism will only get you frightened looks from self-
proclaimed Marx reincarnations. What can you say
about the boring cock-fights between Capitalism deities
of our time? You should be as disgusted as I am of these
clown shows that chip away the substance of economic
disparity dialogues. My rants can turn into a tsunami
but there are events in our lives which, though small,
prove to be very significant.

In transit at the Kenyatta International airport in
Nairobi, Kenya waiting for my flight back to United
States, I was once asked what I wanted to be when I
grow up. The man was sitting right across my table. He
could have been in his late sixties. I could tell by his
features and accent that he was from Rwanda, a nation
that multiple United Nations and other Non-
Governmental watchdog organizations reports have
pointed at being the mastermind of my home country's
political and social horrors. You can understand my rage
after I was briefed on how Rwanda provided financial
and military support to sadistic bandit groups, and, in
return, Rwanda directly plundered Congolese natural
resources and indirectly became a hub for mineral trade.

On that day, I was haunted by one question; how
many blows and lives lost would the Democratic
Republic of Congo have to endure before the world says
enough? With an angry tone, my reply to his question
was audacious and simple: "I want to become a leader in
the Democratic Republic of Congo." While struggling to
suppress his mirth, he asked what would be my

solutions for the DRC. After all, my home country has been through more than half a century of economic and social chaos. At first, I lightheartedly laid down my ideas. He pulled his glasses back and asked me to elaborate more on my plan. Needleless to say, the more I talked the more naïve and dumb I sounded. At the end, I wasn't able to clearly articulate my vision for the reason that I never seriously thought about it in detail. My entire scheme could not stand any scrutiny. The casual conversation turned into a humiliating and humbling experience.

This book emanates from the economic disciplines hijacked by escape artists, and mathematicians, for more than two centuries. For all the wrong reasons, economists have blasted into a million small pieces the Holy Grails of the classical labor theory of value, and stripped away the humanism and the real world from theoretical foundations. Then they took the pain of stitching some of the pieces back, using pathetic assumptions as Band-Aids. There is some truth in the quarantined Marxist, Fred Moseley, charge that the economic academia system has been built to reward folks who stick with the mainstream. This good man is the Shoichi Yokoi of economics, deprived of fame and fortune, hiding in the jungles of South Hadley in Massachusetts, he firmly believed his former comrades would one day return for him, and together they would launch a final assault on Capitalism. Alas, simply castigating orthodoxy for the inaptness of their theory can't restore the classical vision of an efficient market nor get us to the Promised Land.

I kick started this book on a personal note with a letter to Mama Vincent. She is a teenage single mother and panhandler that my wife and I met in downtown Nairobi, Kenya. At one point, I had to hold Vincent in my arms to keep law enforcement agents away. My tourist eminence in Kenya shielded Vincent and his mother from police harassment; the city of Nairobi has passed an ordinance criminalizing poverty instead of raging a war against inequality. This modern era apartheid doesn't call any attention because the oppressed and oppressors have the same skin color. Many more cities are taking the same insane approach and have been getting away with it as long as the line drawn doesn't desecrate the burial of race or ethnic disputes.

In my childhood, I was ingrained with the notion that socio-economic disparity was dictated by law of nature; somebody had to be poor to be a servant of the rich! In the mid-90s, wealthy Congolese sought refuge to the west from the civil war. I stand as a witness to how, in a blink of an eye, most of these families lost their accustomed lifestyle of luxury. After living for close to two decades in exile, even the most powerful generals and the former President's inner circle gradually succumbed to the crippling misery. Not surprisingly, a number of the barons and crusaders of the former regime have crawled back home and are vigorously active in the new parasite system. My wise South African friend referenced a law of nature to explain this cycle: "Once a snake, always a snake!"

The personal testimony is to show the damning universal truth that people as well as nations are more concerned for themselves until their luck changes. This goes for the "Occupy Wall Street," after Americans were shaken out of their dream of a house with a picket fence, and ordinary hardworking Americans saw their pensions completely wiped out by a few greedy vagrants. Another caustic example is the small group of the Russian oligarchy who have since fell out of Vladimir Putin's favor, who can't help but preach fierce justice and equality from their golden exile in London. What is there to say about European countries juggling with mind blowing debt higher than their worth (Gross Domestic Product)? Add to this picture Brazil, Russia, India, and China, the BRIC countries, who are steam-rolling their economic growth at Mother Nature's peril. Added to this gumbo, the Arab majority, who are no longer content with the tiny slice of their national wealth while a minority splurges with the rest, have attempted to shift cards.

These recent bubbling volcanoes should awaken our sense that preemptive measures should be sought to break the status quo. In the twenty-first century, the sluggish economists' speech: "We will be fine as long as we stay on the current course and tweak the old Capitalism wheel a little bit more," has long lost its potency and relevance. It is more than ever imperative to initiate an economic cultural revolution, and to develop a real alternative to the prevailing brutal economic system, which is Capitalism.

The loud medley in my mind bubbled out of the common challenge facing every nation on this dying planet: socio-economic disparity. This is a result of a painful crusade to uncover a pragmatic way in making the gap negligible. Don't pull out your wig yet; I am not totally out of my mind, advocating to jump back on the saddle of any of the two dead horses. Socialism and Communism have failed, but now Capitalism is failing us.

There are a number of elaborate dark labyrinths this book will be taking you through. I firmly believe that economists should leave to religion and medicine, the principal goal of uncovering mysteries of the unnatural and natural while consoling or abusing us on the way. Economics' responsibility is to find remedies for, or to level out, glut and hoarding. Instead, it has been reduced into glorifying socio-economic skewedness.

I have noted the skepticism about whether anything other than Capitalism would ever work. Nowadays, people fail to realize that Capitalism was part of paradigms based on barbaric social norms and practices. Generally, when a social arrangement dominates a field for so long as Capitalism has, it becomes easier to forge that other models, which address different goals and questions, exist or could be constructed. After what we all begin to believe, there is only one way of doing things, and this is the most dangerous lure of all.

Where is the magic book to find out how to break the spell? Like a raging bull, to the disbelief of friends and colleagues, I abruptly interrupted my promising intellectual prostitution career and jumped on what had seemed to be academic vagabondage. My initial objective was to trace the whole commerce system from accounting, finance, management, and end up in economics. As I was delving in the planned last leg of my journey, I was nauseated by economic "gurus" who spent more time claiming incidental correlation to impress the public instead of explaining in a clear concise way economic mechanisms and solving global economic troubles. Regrettably, the laziness of these orators has thwarted the audience's viewpoint. What I can share from my experience with any of you guys who are thinking about questioning today's dominant form of commerce and trade, Capitalism, don't expect an effusive welcome; you should be ready to face the furor of delusional McCarthyists, as I usually do!!!

I have left to the class of economist sloppy cerebral sloths, to tiptoeing around of serious issues. Instead, you, the reader, and I will be swimming against the torrent current. Chapter one through six are exhibits of the case against the current status quo, Capitalism. And if I see you on the other side of chapter seven, please hold my hand tightly from chapter eight through ten. Take your time to digest chapter eleven and get yourself prepared for a big slap to your face. On the closing argument, chapter twelve follows through James Tobin's recommendation: "Good papers in economics contain surprises and stimulate further work."

What else? I made this book easier to read than fat torching. Each chapter debuts with quotes giving you a clue of what to expect and have interjected "interludes" between batches to awaken young readers with short attention spans, and to add a zest of a novel for the literary enthusiasts. I shall confess to folks who expect colorful charts and numbers, and to economists addicted to ketamine (mathematical models), I am sincerely sorry that I have let you down. Yet one thing is for sure, at no time I did pull my punches. Oh yeah, and I did not waste my energy on the discourse of 20th century economists. You do no need to sample manure in order to confirm it is manure; the stench of falsehoods is sufficient to discern it as such.

The idea of writing a book is liken to getting butt naked in front of a large audience; I never had a problem doing that. But my constant inner battles through this experience consisted of synchronizing my heart with my mind. This is to say that I had to overcome the temptation of being guided solely by either passion or vision, both intensity and accuracy are essential in this enterprise to birth out a pertinent central concept. Remember, in life, passion without vision is a waste of energy, and vision without passion is a dead-end.

One brilliant soul often chanted: "Swami Vivekananda put it so eloquently: Take up one idea. Make that one idea your life – think of it, dream of it, live on that idea. Let the brain, muscles, nerves, every part of your body, be full of that idea, and just leave every other idea alone. This is the way to success." The world might one day know the magnitude of sacrifices I made to cultivate this idea I truly care about, a solution to the severe global socio-economic inequality. Yet the anchor of this book would be in vain without providing a full-bodied alternative to Capitalism, a remedy that might justly mend *Thomas Piketty's misfire*. It is about time that we bring back dialectic analysis without channeling economic old demons. Above all, I hope this book will stimulate a number of people to discuss and further the solution proposed in this book, or to

creatively give life to another path away from
Capitalism. And may *William Godwin* rest, at last, in
peace.

II

Kamikaze

"I am the wisest man alive, for I know one thing, and
that is I know nothing."

Socrates

A few years back, while I was walking down a
cluttered and depressing street of Addis Ababa in
Ethiopia, the sight of a frail teenage mother and
a sleeping filthy child wrapped on her back with a little
piece of cloth instantly transported my mind back to my
intellectual "Waterloo" defeat at Kenyatta International
airport in Nairobi. It was then that it hit me, Eureka!
Still, on that day, I was far from years of an
investigative roller coaster ride to articulate clearly a
cure for the social class decomposition tormenting every
society.

After that I invested time, money, and energy to
get a real sense of the problems facing people around the
globe. To that end, Tara and I traveled as much as we
could afford, read abundantly, and were glued for hours
to the television screen watching documentaries. One of
my crusades took us across the Sub-Saharan and

Eastern region of Africa (SSEA), and we were astonished by the region's many challenges which transcend geographical boundaries. The overriding feature of the countries of SSEA is an exotic mamba with two heads: corruption, and repression. You can blame the region's dysfunctional governments which are essentially being used as an apparatus to consolidate power and wealth within a few ruling families. In short, public services across SSEA are in a shamble.

Yet there are a lot of fingers to be pointed around for the SSEA's organized chaos; these extremely poor management practices are either of the SSEA nations' own design or imposed on them from outside, as I suspect, to impede both internal and regional development. And while touring different cities in the western hemisphere, I noted the same gangrene as I find in African or Latin American countries. You would think that the state of Illinois was in Nigeria when the former Governor Rod Blagojevich was sent behind bars for trying to sell the forty fourth President of United States, Barack Obama, former senatorial seat. And BRIC reported scandals are of epic proportion. I am not a big fan of fútbol, but I expected Brazilian contractors to make a mockery of the 2014 soccer World Cup, with overpriced stadiums and bridges that crumbled before and during the sacred festivity. And I don't know what to say about the scandal in China's southern city of Hengyang that triggered the resignation of almost the entire city's People's Congress leaders. The prevalence of resource mismanagement and leaders' self-indulgence have resulted in globally unprecedented levels of financial waste.

"A casual stroll through the lunatic asylum shows
that faith doesn't prove anything."

Wilhelm Nietzsche

On my tour du poor monde, I met dedicated westerner
students who were on, or getting ready for, mission trips
to spice up their resumes or who wanted to boost up
their chances to be admitted in a prestigious higher
learning institution. I have caught myself glazing over
by beautiful pictures of A-listed celebrities, or a charity
spokesperson, who profoundly wanted to 'save the
people' (though sometimes the animals more than the
people). Yet, the madness is nothing compared to
graduate classes on public engagement and economic
development that I have taken on the better side of the
globe, where I found people who see themselves as
miracle laborers and benefactors of third world
countries. As talented as these individuals might be, the
flaws in their conceptual approach is the bigoted view of
less developed nations' challenges and needs. They based
their models of development on the deep rooted passion
for Capitalism. This mindset reminded me of the
aphorism "if the only tool you have is a hammer,
everything starts to look like a nail."

What is more hazardous to poor nations than smart
ass westerners? Immigrants from god forgotten
countries; self-enslaved and adoring conformists, with
the little access to modern amenities that they've
acquired, who dare vocalize that living on a dollar a day
is "just how it is" in their home countries. I have found a
high concentration of these stupid individuals in

England, where Engel's account of the living conditions only a century ago send chills down my spine. And in the United States, which was not long ago a shit hole with a putrid stench of racism, sexism, and a world of bigotry (some of the stench still lingers around). Lastly, if you are one of those monkeys from a repressive authoritarian regime who is walking down a lit up street in the west, delighted from the addictive sense of protection and freedom and yet has a firm conviction that poor nations need a "strong man" for peace and development? Before you read the rest of the book, repent!!!

It has to be noted that throughout time, a dominant society has always knighted itself the prestigious 'exceptionalism' status. I would applaud this gut and bravura if their economists take up the leadership responsibilities of dissecting accurately the world around and, accordingly, prescribe effective interventions that would lift us all up. What do we have right now? A total fuming global mess where cost-effective and Gross Domestic Product (an insane way to gauge development) are at the center of leading initiatives. And I have to underline the over used excuse, "globalization", since it has added elements of scope and speed to the mix. What to say about mankind when, time and time again, leading nations turn a blind eye on the imposition of inhumane practices, which at one time was slavery in past centuries, and now is self-enslavement, as long as it benefits them?

I get angry when westerners are surprised that these development programs, which are shoved down the throats of problematic countries, do not lead to prophesized outcomes. I become angrier when solutions for inhabitants' needs can be addressed in an integrated way, but from their desks in Washington, DC, economic druids clean the data up and develop simplified models which abstract from the complexity of observable reality. Critical studies conducted by no other than International Monetary Fund (IMF) and World Bank insiders have poured out questioning the effectiveness of the main international financial institutions' programs. These guilty consciences decry how a country economically faint is treated as a coma, and rushed into an international organization emergency room, and locked into unplugged financial incubators, knocked out by an addictive overdose of aid, is then molested and gangbanged by frantic necrophiliacs, and used as a testing ground for irrational experimental reform programs. God forbid, a vegetated nation shows any sign of life after these unnecessary open heart surgeries as Argentina did, it will be at the mercy of ferocious vultures who would try to pull its eyeballs and intestines out.

What is the common antidote injected into a nation once deemed as a 'failed state'? Let's look at Haiti, after hurricane Sandy blasted through this voodoo nation that was already wobbling for a century. First, it was quarantined and put under the spooky eyes of an international trusteeship. After what powerful nations imposed with *douceur* (democratic elections) to millions of illiterates a charismatic buffoon whose brightest idea is to organize carnival celebrations all over the smaller portion of the island of Hispaniola while serious decisions were taken solely by the World Bank and International Monetary Fund emissaries. Haiti was far from being an isolated case, international assistance funds have been used to extract the sort of concessions that crippled nations are often not willing to make in healthy times.

What we have seen in Haiti, and other black holes where those same approaches were taken, is that remedies produced a worse net result than the problem did. Primarily because these nations' kleptomaniacs and technical 'partners' often implement contradictory dogmas and reforms that caused poor countries to fall further behind. I should not be the first one to tell you that John Maynard Keynes and Harry Dexter White's offspring, and other international financial institutions, act at the whim of their backers and backers' backers' interests. This, in turn, leads to another round of resource waste and mismanagement. And if you are craving to get a sense of the magnitude of this mess, please take a tour of Cite' Jalousie, Port au Prince, Haiti and compare it to villas rented by United Nations 'peacemakers'.

> "I preached as never sure to preach again, and as a dying man to dying men."
>
> Richard Baxter

Nowadays, economists claim that a theory can't be developed except in a purely numb way; any phenomenon that can't be reconstructed in a mathematical model is deemed illogical and trashed. If in a sense, nothing is explained unless everything is stated in a mind-bending equation frame, this book is read as a suicidal letter. Yet, I am not depressed enough either to jump in front of a subway train or to make a journey to a Buddhist monk temple. I have to thank the classical and prodigal economists who were not inclined in this constraint and who aesthetically birthed eminent principles and, in most cases, robust diabolic treatises.

In third world countries, the contrast between the misery and despair of the many and the level of opulence and waste of the few is not a complex abstract, but rather an observable reality on a global scale amounting to a moral abomination. Western revisionists are suggesting that third world countries' nightmares have nothing to with the colonization when we see post-colonial social layers mirroring the caste system inherited from colonization's ruthless exploitive method. And little has it done, other than imposing a maniac head of state, to help the marginalized evade a bleak future. This is to say, economic cannibalism (Capitalism) doesn't fit developing countries' realities and potentials.

In the global Capitalism arena, a nation's ability to race against others of at least the same size, predetermines its prospect for growth and development. The Republic of Burundi and the Kingdom of Belgium, two countries of roughly the same size and population, cannot be further apart economically. Burundi's GDP is two hundred times less then Belgium. Other than racking debt higher than the tiny Kingdom's GDP, how else did Belgium achieve this prowess? Well, we need to turn to historical facts to explain Belgium's *comparative advantage* over Burundi. The Kingdom had adopted a

cruel method to amass its national wealth. While
Germans were decimating Burundi's socio-culture
structures, from 1887 to1965, King Leopold II of
Belgium, and subsequently Belgium as a nation, was
sadistically plundering wealth from a territory eighty
times its size, known today as the "Democratic" Republic
of Congo. And After World War II, Burundi was
wrenched from Germany's grip and given to Belgium by
the League of Nations for enduring a lucid form of
colonization by their big neighbor.

It is worth noting however, that poor countries are
not my sole sources of evidence of the global mess. On
the one hand, centralized economies have failed by
imposing a uniform basket of needs on people, stranding
ninety-nine percent at the bottom. The defunct Soviet
Union implemented perfectly Communism until it hit a
wall, literally. Whereas on the other hand, the free
market is failing us with an unethical rule of the
survival of the fittest, catering to a small group of the
one percent on the top. The only time, in recent
memories, The United States congress came together in
bipartisan fashion was to bail out numerous 'too big to
fail' US banks and insurance companies. In contrast, in
2013, the same congress slashed billions of dollars from
the food stamp program that had kept a chunk of The
United States population's noses above the poverty level.

When you pay attention to the global financial
transactions postcard, you should be able to see how the
Capitalism model has confined the major lucrative
international financial flows within the same economies.
Other countries are reduced to mere providers of raw
material and cheaper labor. But the fat lady is about to

stop singing very soon, she is getting too plump to stand longer on her feet. In 2010, General Motors shut down their plant in Antwerp, Belgium because of the excess capacity in the European car industry. Subsequently, other plants across different industries in Europe and North America have since closed their doors.

"Koketsu ni irazunba koji wo ezu."
Japanese wisdom

Although by respective economic doctrine, Cuba and England are recklessly doing right. At the assessment of the two existing economic lines of attacks (poverty, pollution, war, etc...) suggests to our sense of humanity that neither approaches is the right thing to do. I had a glimmer of hope when the former Soviet Union and China decided to go cold turkey, breaking out from the communist penitentiary institution, until they ran straight into the psychiatric Capitalism facility which is a pure form of insanity!

Currently, the world lacks full-bodied alternatives and, after multiple frantic financial crises, acknowledging Capitalism's flaw shouldn't be profane. And in the light of recurrent facts financial cataclysms either austerity or spending, has shown not to be a sustainable solution, but rather a lampooning of the struggling class. I allow myself here to say in the most simplistic way, new markets need to be promoted to rejuvenate the global economic system, but in doing so, new trends need to be developed to avoid the final cataclysm. This change requires to apply the appropriate economic form that will not only move 'poor' countries into the international trade system, as to say from exploited bystanders to active producers and consumers, but also break current markets' affairs from the old order.

Creative as mankind is, I used to wait on the side for a superwoman to save us all. Then I learned that in 1945, when American and British battleships and aircraft carriers were getting close to the Japanese mainland, ordinary young people were asked to make the ultimate sacrifice to save the empire of the rising sun; their lives. The pitch of victimhood built on the atomic attacks on Hiroshima and Nagasaki romanticized these young men's fearlessness. I took an offense when called a kamikaze for my attacks on Capitalism only after I learned about the Nanjing Massacre, and women forced into sex slavery for the Japanese military.

Tired of waiting for a whistle that will halt our self-imposed destruction, I am not going to bore you with the same crybaby wailing that you have come to associate with critics of Capitalism. To bust your bubbles, the solution is neither increasing minimum wage nor a building up of tax barracks. These two are nothing more than economic palliative remedies. To your delight or indignation, I am going to expose your few remaining neurons to a new economic form that potentially transposes general notions by propelling the ninety nine to the top and take care of the one percent less fortunate at the bottom. And Caesar, ahem, you the reader, would have to decide my fate!

III

I see poor people

"In a country well governed, poverty is something to be ashamed of. In a country badly governed, wealth is something to be ashamed of."

Confucius

In my view, by far the creepiest social site out there is one dedicated to M. Night Shyamalan by one of his diehard followers. For an Indian-American to achieve such a high level of success as a screenwriter, film producer and director, and A-listed star of Hollywood without relying on the clichéd dancing and chanting Bollywood cinematographic format, is impressive. I am, myself, a huge fan of his breakthrough and most celebrated movie, *The Sixth Sense* (1999). This movie's box office gross suggests that there are not many homo-sapiens who haven't watched it; for the rest of you who were still living in cages around that time, the superb plot is around a boy, Cole, who has the ability to communicate with spirits that don't know they are dead. He seeks the help of a depressed child psychologist, a role superbly played by one of

Hollywood's biggest stars at the time, Bruce Willis. The movie's good bumping moment comes when the camera zooms slowly in to the boy's face, then-unknown child actor Haley Joel Osment, and he whispers: "I see dead people", turning the line instantly into one of the most used catchphrases of that time.

It has been quite some time since I found myself entangled in a dilemma similar to Cole's. No doubt that the crusade I have embarked on has drawn me to experience life as I never thought I would. Let me assure you, the life of a hermit monk hasn't sounded appealing to me, yet. But I have to say that the emotional expedition has broken my myopic life lenses which forced me to observe my surroundings, relying on all of my senses and upped my state of consciousness. After enlisting new priorities in my daily life, nowadays, I have a hard time sleeping all through the night and my mind flies miles away in the middle of dull seminars and conversations. When you have voices nagging in your head, pointing left and right, life becomes a wild roller coaster ride. I came to wonder when the devil had possessed me!? And I can't afford to hire my own disheartened shrink, even less Bruce Willis (I tried). In the goal of exorcizing my demons, I hope that pinning down critical events in my ordinary life will help trace the original trigger that led to my obsession of caring for the less fortunate; I cannot stop seeing poor people!!!

Tara's parents, Haitian immigrants, ran away from the hard knock life of New York City to raise their newly born child in The United States retirement epicenter, south Florida. From the time Tara and I met, she was boiling to reverse her parents' migration cycle and talked my ears off about the "Big Apple". When you add to my wife's inducement strategy the list of egotistic New Yorkers I had met in Florida, you start imagining the city as if it was the land of milk and honey; a nirvana where opportunities and excitement are waiting on every corner. It came as a huge disappointment to my wife that we didn't move to her dream city, but rather into a quaint little town in Massachusetts. Ironically, I commuted routinely to New York City for school. The graduate program I matriculated into was situated smack dab in Manhattan, right in the mix of historic skyscrapers and not far from the around-the-clock and year-long tourist infected Times Square. Learning from my experience, I have to caution people out there dying to get a long bite of the "Big Apple", before moving up north, to scrutinize diligently the madness older and rich folks are running away from.

New York City is home to the world's boldest financial delinquents, the New York Stock Exchange and NASDAQ, and to the most mishandled international organization headquarters, the United Nations. With an estimated Gross Domestic Product higher than Saudi Arabia, and almost twice that of Switzerland, it has had a billionaire as a mayor, Michael Bloomberg, bigger than life multi-millionaire unofficial mayor of the negroes in the city, Sean John Combs aka Puff Daddy, and everything glamorous publicized about the Broadway theater district and ostentatiously expensive Bergdorf Goodman department store, let's ignore for a moment the city's rodent problem and bloodbaths in Brownsville, Brooklyn, but why is the city not able to take care of the poor? As I pushed amongst the crowds, the seemingly too busy to stay still, what I kept bumping into on every corner were the beleaguered faces of the poor. It truly bugs me how a city of flamboyant super wealthy characters like Donald Trump, is not able to find a human solution for its less fortunate, as the trickle-down theory suggests.

I find it torturous walking out of the New York City central station, dodging the overlooked mentally ill, and avoiding eye contact with those who are laying on the floor. This morose spectacle has turned me into a good priest passing the Eucharist, in my case, my lunch money. When winter came, I realized that there were fewer and fewer beggars around my usual crucifixion path. At last, I could get a decent meal without the burning guilty sentiment lodged in my gut. Yet, I was unable to silence my suspicions for long and questioned where the lava of homeless had gone that I had become accustomed to. In reality, no miracle had happened, just the weather. As ol'man winter made its grim appearance, the homeless try to find warm shelters and, inevitably, have to retreat into invisibility.

In 2013, alarming news emerged of the spike on the number of homeless arriving in shelters and due to housing's limited capacities, adults and children alike had to be turned away every night. What to say about the number of US veterans who are homeless? If the United States, currently ranked as the wealthiest nation on Earth, doesn't move Heaven and Earth to care for those who have answered the call to honorably serve the country and abandon noble beings who have put their life at risk to protect the nation, I can't think about anyone else it can show empathy to.

And while I am on the subject of empathy, the World Bank estimates that 54 percent of Mumbai residents live in slums. The "Slumdog Millionaire" is how most people of the western world got a sense of life in Mumbai, and several scenes from the movie were recorded there. Mumbai is a city of contrasts, it is also home to some of the country's wealthiest businessmen and Bollywood film stars. I can't help but wonder if the archaic caste system and deep-rooted religious faith have made the common Indian susceptible to accept disparity in their society as a work of divine force; destiny. I could not find any public outcry against the Indian space program's (I.S.R.O) budget gradually boosted up to $1.3 billion in 2013. The 2013 I.S.R.O. budget figures triggered countries such as India's former colonial power, the United Kingdom, and one of the nation's best buddies, the United States, to cut aid fund to India. The amount is evidently small compared to the I.S.R.O budget, but it was a huge hit taken by diverse programs that provided needed services to an estimated 421 million of the Indian poor. This number is higher than the 410 million poor living in the 26 poorest African nations. And what was India's response to the aid cut? "We don't really need the aid", said P. Chidambaram, India's finance minister at the time.

In November 2013, my Indian-American friends celebrated when India's space program confirmed that the Mars Orbiter had debuted the planned ten month journey. The Indian Mars probe has raised some of my

deepest suspicion... it was actually orbiting the Earth
for some time. I imagine that Indian scientists got
depressed looking at Indian slums, and decided to turn
their telescopes away. Is the mission's real goal to find a
new hide-out for the Indian elite or a dump/final solution
for the poor of places like the slums of Mumbai? If it
happens to be the latter, the few clauses on the ratified
agreement between the Federal Republic of Nigerian
and Indian space programs regarding slums scattered
around Abuja should be fascinating!

Now try to Google the most expensive house in the
world's history; surprisingly, it is not located in
Manhattan nor anywhere in Paris, but it is in Mumbai,
India and is valued at more than $1 billion USD! The
twenty-seven story skyscraper has six underground
parking levels, one level dedicated to a health center and
requires about 600 staff for its maintenance. This
gargantuan residence is home to the Indian billionaire,
Mukesh Ambani, his wife, two sons and a daughter. It
doesn't pain me as much that in a nation where many
children go hungry and live in slums as much as he
chose to spend a billion dollars building his residence on
a land owned previously by an orphanage. The land was
allocated for the purpose of educating underprivileged
children. I guess that he wanted to have a beautiful view
of the city, and its slums.

Talking about a beautiful view, the Gulf of Florida
has some of the most immaculate beaches on the planet.
Anyone who desires an urban lifestyle and quick access
to splendid beaches, the city of Tampa is the right place
to live because of its proximity to the coastal city of Saint
Petersburg. Now, any tourist is going to have a nice time

wandering around under the caressing sun, tasting some authentically fattening American gourmet at the center of the town, and stopping by the beach for an ice cream. Once the sun goes down, it is advisable for any caring soul to avoid venturing within distance of the city center. I have found myself downtown late at night, waiting for the Greyhound bus to take me back to Tampa. I swear, criminality is not what people have to worry about. The upsurge of homeless laying their boxes down, trying to find a shelter around the imposing local Catholic Church building and the center park is heartbreaking. Adding to that humiliation, the homeless are constantly being harassed by the police on patrol, enforcing what I call a zero-tolerance of the poor decree passed by the local council. As a tactic to get rid of the poor, once arrested and released, they are given a Greyhound ticket out of Saint Petersburg to any destination of their choice, which is usually Tampa. I do think it is one of the most creative and diabolic measures taken in the goal of safeguarding the city's quixotic image.

When somebody says quixotic image, for some reason my mind centers on the city of Burma, officially the Republic of the Union of Myanmar. My enchanting depiction was, for a long time, the result of a leaked video of the General Than Shwe's daughter wedding in 2006. There were strings of diamonds and tons of champagne bottles on display. It was estimated that she received tens of millions of dollars' worth of gifts, including luxury cars and houses. I can remember being so envious of the groom, watching him pouring champagne over a cascade of glasses and helping his

bride slice into a huge wedding cake. At the news of
Aung San Su Kyi being released from house arrest in
November 2010, I took a second look at the video and did
some research. On the video, the smiling guests,
wrapped in the finest clothing and expensive jewels,
were all part of a brutal and sanguinary military
leadership who had an iron-clad grip on the country.
This opulent party is happening while Burma's level of
poverty and military repression continued to rise. The
military junta has since gone through a strategic
renovation. The surgical changes are noticeable; these
tigers have adopted formal civilian outfits. But their
sincerity is questionable. The ruling elite members are
still the same. I really don't see them relinquishing
control over the Burmese military forces which is
unmistakably the source their control over the country
and its vast resources. So far, the charm offensive
appears to be working. Yangon international airport is
busy again rolling out a red carpet on the step of world
power brokers and their squads of financial crooks' jets.
No doubt in my mind that parties will go on for some
time again, although in secret.

This got me wondering, what has happened to the
most exhilarating party in United States that was no
secret by any means? In 2003, getting "fresh off of the
boat", as many of my American compadres would label a
Caribbean and African newcomer like myself, I came
across a brochure of "Mardi Gras" events in New
Orleans, Louisiana, jam-packed with images of young
folks partying and with delightful praises of bayou
gastronomy. A couple of friends and I couldn't wait to
cash in a bunch of coupons stacked into the booklet.

Needless to say, we drove down to the 'Big Easy' as fast
and drunk as we could. Miraculously, we did not end up
on some chain-gang in Mississippi. The food and the
hospitality on Bourbon Street were outstanding. And
more importantly, only few party musketeers could
boast that every one of their notorious Bourbon Street
rituals were a triumph. Let's just say that each time we
left the hotel with hundreds of beads, following the
festivities' sacrosanct tradition, we stumbled back to our
room with empty hands...wink, wink!

On our way back to Florida, with our minds still
floating in the sky, we missed the ramp to the Hale
Boggs Bridge over the Mississippi River. Anyone who
has been to New Orleans knows that the bridge is the
only way of getting out of the city. There was no need to
panic until we realized why the hotel concierge
instructions were to avoid, at any cost, venturing outside
the touristic parameter which is roughly around the
French Quarter. Oh, Lord! For the first time on our
sojourn in New Orleans, the décor was of concern. We all
sobered up fast. It is not far-fetched to say, if the police
had tried to pull us over, they would have had to follow
us back on Bourbon Street. We weren't about to make
any stop in the middle of that jungle.

To get an idea of our ragtag group, we were raised
watching the black family on the Cosby show series,
scenes of New York City in Eddie Murphy's comedy hit
'Coming to America' was too surreal to be true for us. In
other words, we were from predominantly affluent
families that got more than a justifiable share of wealth
in the Capitalism 'a *l'africaine'* system. Even though we

had a considerable number of black American acquaintances back in Tallahassee, Florida, which is a classic college town and a serene state capital, those Negroes in N'awlins and the surrounding projects scared the hell out of all of us! We should have known that something was fishy about this city. New Orleans produced one of the most prolific rap groups that we loved at the time, the 'Hot Boyz'. Their creative rap prose, raw style and catch phrases cannot obviously come from a place of joy and kumbayah; rather, it's from a sanctuary of pain and desperation. If that red flag wasn't visible enough, the group's initial low budget music videos gave a tour of their world, a cornucopia of dirt-ass poor people in front of poorly maintained public housing blocks.

Sadly, these days, some opt to ignore or chose to forget the fact that way before the devastating hurricane Katrina swept through the city, New Orleans had some of the shittiest places in the United States comparable to parts of third world countries I have traveled to. As my friends and I came to find out, those shameful pockets of the 'Big Easy' were superbly tucked away, out of the view of the drunken college students and other tourists. Hurricane Katrina simply flushed out the city's filthy secret, and the entire United States pretended to be surprised. Really, what else do you expect when a sanitary sewer overflows? And now that the chocolate city, as it was called by then New Orleans Mayor Ray Nagin (sentenced ten years in prison for bribery, money laundering and other corruption), is rebuilding, it probably is praying for its problems to never come back,

wishing it could declare a section of its former residents
persona non grata.

'Persona non grata' might not be clearly stated on
the city of New Orleans' Christmas wish list; but it has
been Teodoro Nguema Obiang, the son of Equatorial
Guinea President, status in France and in most civilized
nations. France got exasperated by the Negro prince's
opulence and in 2012, it was reported that French police
suddenly decided to act on a past lawsuit brought by
different activist organizations and took away a couple of
Obiang Jr.'s toys. The subsequent viewing of all the
baubles pictured on French magazines surpassed my
imagined *folie de grandeur* among the eleven luxury cars
(two Bugatti Veyrons, a Maybach, an Aston Martin, a
Ferrari Enzo, a Ferrari 599 GTO, a Rolls-Royce
Phantom, and a Maserati MC12), plus some bottles
Château Pétrus (among the world's most expensive
wines) and a $3.7 million clock.

Not one to be outdone by the French, the Americans
attempted to put a bigger dent on Obiang Jr.'s fortune.
The public got blitzed with news that the United States
Justice Department filed a $70 million forfeiture action
against Obiang Jr. And voilà, another list that included
a Gulfstream jet, Michael Jackson's infamous gloves,
and a villa in Malibu, California. But wait a minute! The
kid was still allowed to parade around huge amounts of
money in the United States after the scandal that forced
the Riggs Bank to shut down? Somehow, the United
States Justice Department never troubled the bank's
largest single depositor at the time, with over $700
million. What is there to make of all of this juicy story?

By no stretch of the imagination, the very young Teodoro Nguema Obiang has presumably amassed all of that uncovered fortune while earning a salary of less than $100,000 per year as Equatorial Guinea's minister of Agriculture and Forestry.

What can be said about Equatorial Guinea to put everything in perspective; the country is among the most repressed countries in West Africa, and if we take the proportion of its people living on less than a dollar a day, it is also among the poorest. This nation of just 700,000 people is at the same time poverty-stricken and oil-rich, a contrast of epic proportions. There are pictures on social media sites of glassy high rises and presidential mansions next to rusted shacks. As one visits the country's capital Malabo, there are sightings of people riding in flashy Mercedes Benzes through the slums and trying to miss the city's zillion potholes and of the country's chief of police, who is related to the president, bragging that his uniforms are tailored by none other than the French celebrated designer, Yves Saint Laurent. From the fancy room's window of the brand new hotel he stayed in, he could see families crammed into small and tin-roofed shacks.

And while I was digging out more facts, like one out five children dies before reaching the age of five years old and less than fifty percent have access to clean drinkable water, I was stunned to learn that the commissioner of police of a tiny country located right in the center of Mandela's Rainbow nation, was presenting, on behalf of his greedy and perverted absolute monarch, a sincere apology for two million Euros stolen, strangely in a briefcase, during a party in Obiang Jr.'s villa in

Swaziland. If anyone is wondering, what about Teodoro
Nguema Obiang's punishment for exhibiting such
extravagance and tarnishing Equatorial Guinea's image?
Well, let's say that it fits a son of one of Africa's longest-
ruling dictators, a shrinking elite group. His father has
since made him Second Vice President of Equatorial
Guinea; this highly regarded and guarded position,
shielding him from any eventual international
prosecution.

"I am for doing good to the poor, but I differ in
opinion about the means. I think the best way of doing
good to the poor is not making them easy in poverty, but
leading or driving them out of it."

Benjamin Franklin

Noah was a good man, but he is to blame for spoiling my
childhood's unique way of escaping abuses at home.
After a neighboring kid's dramatic incident in our
home's backyard, I got terrified to play Rambo camping
out by myself. I have long suspected that Noah had
something to do with my tactic fiasco; the detail of his
exploit brought up irrefutable evidence of his guilt. I
have read different versions of Noah's Ark story, and it
all boiled down to the same specifics; Noah saved
himself, his family, and a remnant of all the world's
animals when God decided to flood the world, and
destroy it because of humanity's evil deeds. As a child, I
found this so reprehensible that the unsupervised Noah
chose, among other animals, to also allow on board,
vultures, rats, crocodiles, and particularly the biblical

source of Adam and Eve's demise, and my childhood summer long caging, I'm talking about snakes.

Parallel to Noah's Ark story, Mandela was also a good man. Then again, he ruined something so dear to me. I have dreamed of spending my golden age in the wealthiest and inspiring African country, South Africa 'SA', a plausible way of enjoying my retirement amongst prosperous black Africans. In the past couple of years, I couldn't quite figure out Mandela's responsibility in my fading dream. Ultimately when I set aside the fact he spent 27 years in a labor camp for his part in the struggle against Apartheid and then critically reassessed his one term as president of SA, it got crystal clear. I consider myself a member of the tiny bold group navigating uncharted territories and whose voices should have preferably been louder before 'Madiba's' death; do we dare denounce that South Africa's socio-economic woes were perpetuated by the 'compromised negotiations'? There is no doubt in my mind that Mandela got a great deal for himself, ANC & Co., and the small affluent white society when F.W. de Klerk who, in my view, bears some resemblance as God, is a white old man and undertone racist, was pressed to bring to an end to Apartheid by white South African middle class and big businesses burgeoning dissatisfactions in the 1990s.

I have succumbed to my grandparents' mantra that people should be judged solely by their actions; two real facts put into question Mandela's strength of character. The unchecked 'Madiba' went too far to accommodate the apartheid establishment by striking a deal with racist judges, some of the worst human rights violators, the Afrikaner squads of kidnappers and murderers and exclusively the ones who sponsored the entire Apartheid cruel system and who have become the modern safeguard of the rainbow elite; I am pointing at the mining and financial corporations. And what's to say about a man who in an interview with the Australian reporter John Pilger, expressed a total disregard toward Indonesia's three decades long brutal dictatorship and other people struggling alike, who went on to justify rewarding in 1997 the Butcher of Jakarta, General Suharto, with the Order of Good Hope, which is South Africa's highest honor that could be bestowed on a foreigner?

I can't reconcile the fact that The African National Congress (ANC), South Africa's national liberation movement and their allies have won all of the South African presidential elections since the end of Apartheid. And yet, the de facto economic apartheid remains intact. South African blacks remain horrifically poor in absolute and relative terms. To my eyes, the ANC has abused the trust of black people who are still cramped in slums like Dimbaza and Alexandria, and these violent townships are beginning to bear the brunt of popular frustration. In contrast, there is plenty of evidence that the ANC has been good for the whites. In exchange for including a few ANC black operatives in their glamorous closed circle (a scheme used to funnel money back into affluent party members' pockets), whites in SA have been allowed to enjoy discreetly behind massive barricades, the wealth extracted and amassed from the inhumane exploitation of blacks in SA during the Apartheid. Another way to say it is when the South African apartheid was choked, their leaders realized that all they had to do is bring black leaders in the business of distributing wealth and welfare, and the explosive greed disintegrated the ability of Negroes and Indians to act collectively across neighborhoods and ghettoes.

I once asked myself how Mandela & Co. planned to lead or drive black South Africans out of poverty?! One would find that the ANC set a great map plan to that end, stating unmistakably in a segment of the Party's Freedom Charter:

"The national wealth of our country, the heritage of South Africans, shall be restored to the people; The mineral wealth beneath the soil, the banks and monopoly industry shall be transferred to the ownership of the people as a whole; All other industry and trade shall be controlled to assist the wellbeing of the people..."

This section of the ANC's Freedom Chart is inconsistent with concessions that they made such as the late 1992 "sunset clauses". It paved the way for a Government of National Unity (dictators' favorite method to blend wolves and lambs together and to diffuse popular demand for change), and for the absurd job guarantees that protect all Apartheid-era civil servants.

And if one wonders in the post-Apartheid era what happens when poor blacks take it upon themselves and demand an adequate share of the nation's wealth? The awful truth is that the response has been the same as it was under Apartheid; they get gunned down like rabid dogs. The footage that circulated of the Marikana massacre of miners in 2013 were no different to the

Sharpeville massacre in 1960. Only this time, the images were in color and the inhuman job was done by colored police officers. Adding to the insult, the world was stunned to learn that 270 miners were arrested and charged for murder on the basis of the doctrine of "common purpose", the same doctrine set, used, and abused under Apartheid. Due to the outcry of human rights watch groups and international pressure, the bizarre charge was dropped, and all imprisoned miners were released.

Mandela's life and ANC ascension should be a cautionary tale for aspiring freedom fighters and individuals haunted by the belief of equality around the globe; power corrupts and absolute power corrupts absolutely as Lord Acton fittingly surmised. It pains me to see in SA that, with time, the gap between the white and blacks "have none" has reached the highest level. Indeed in 2009, SA sidelined Brazil as the most skewed society in the world. Nonetheless, I took pleasure watching the SA President Jacob Zuma getting humiliated in front of foreign dignitaries during none other than Mandela's memorial, people's expression of their discontent of the ANC! It was so moving.

In 2013, my wife and I moved from the sunny southern part of the United States to somewhere close to freezing Canada. The best ethnic description of this charming little town: a black ghost town. We always felt obligated to acknowledge, and at the same time, to rejoice in the presence of another black person by nodding our heads to one another. Being used to down south, where Negroes populate a considerable chunk of the society hierarchy bottom, I naively thought that any traceable strong smell of decaying poverty couldn't be found around here. Then came thanksgiving 2013, we were on our way to New York City when there suddenly appeared a shadow in the middle of the road. There, battling the gruesome freezing temperature and slightly covered, was a homeless white man branding a big sign. And gosh, senseless drivers almost ran him over. As we got closer, I pulled my window down to give him a dollar bill. Something shifted inside of me because I saw the face of a man humiliated and broken. On that day, from that point on, I kept seeing the same expression on a child, a woman, or another man on different corners.

Cities have found that changing the reflection of a word is the clever way of expressing the disdain of a certain group. Adding a negative twist to panhandling has permitted towns to chastise the poor. Around this beautiful planet what is called "aggressive" panhandling is prohibited. Some towns have even gone so far as to actively conducting educational outreach programs to residents, advising them not to give to moochers (sorry, label borrowed from the 2012 Republican Party's nominee for President of the United States, Mitt Romney); and their police departments have been instructed to bully panhandlers, especially around the downtown zones. Poor countries are more creative; they have added the supernatural element or voodoo to the pretexts. While touring several third world countries, paranoid guides and friends always warned me not to give money to street beggars, and if I ever dare, supposedly, money will mysteriously disappear from my pockets and I would have brought some juju curse on myself. But I did laugh at, and broke this ridiculous rule. I can testify that I didn't turn into a goat or was struck by lightning, and all my money's disappearance has been accounted for by my pursuits of materialistic happiness.

It is deplorable that people around the world from different ways of life, race, and background would bluntly say that they hate active solicitation, or aggressive panhandling, but they don't mind passive panhandling of which an example is opening doors at the store with a cup in hand but saying nothing. As to say, people are comfortable to give when beggars don't bother our conscience and make their presence less felt. I have taken my time to watch cool kids rushing through New York City's central station exit with the latest super expensive Dr. Dre brand line of headphones covering more than their ears, and government officials speeding through the bumpy and dusty roads of Kampala, Uganda on brand new black-tinted 4x4 Prados, without any of them noticing the poor on the corner. These spectacles brought me to the realization that the indefensible and heartless attitude toward the less fortunate is truly an omnipresent global phenomenon. Yet, when I find myself outnumbered and starting to lose hope, I always come across another batch set of individuals on this beautiful blue planet from diverse ways of life, race and background. Unlike popular academic charlatans who simply brush off the poverty issue to get a certain academic notoriety, they dedicate their lives to break the momentum of the indifference towards the poor. I find this sentiment very moving and it echoes the deeper desires of my own heart; a decent society doesn't happen miraculously. As I do (I guess), they can't stop seeing poor people.

Interlude II

It seem like every time I will get to your side

Something will be going crazy inside

Fearing the mother of all detonation

Glory is just a tool for self-humiliation

Pearls shinning from mars

Vision of diving in splendid stars

Lovers sinking in ugly cars

Caught that immense intriguing fire in flight

Flush but feeling like a tombstone

Heart shield from a beautiful invasion

Rats climbing on the headstone

Doves throwing gems and gold

Snakes looking happily lost in the cold

Monkeys swinging on any root that can hold

Caught that intense melancholic fire in life

Dove can't anymore fly away

While the magic going away

Hoping to grow wings again on day

It shall no more fly on your bay

Overstretched royal arrogance

Xenophobic sacred ambiance

Tragedy waiting for the last dance

Naughty thoughts poisoning the cadence

Caught that sparkly tragic fire in line

If you have not got it by now

Turn down your light now

Find the particular call now

Reveal what you experience now

Caught that severe miserable fire in my mind

IV

Gangnam Style

"Every time we buy something we deepen our emotional deprivation and hence our need to buy something."

Philip Slater

If the first time you saw Psy humping around in a shiny tuxedo and sunglasses was on Saturday Night Live, also known as "SNL", the popular American comedy show, you probably assumed it was a parody based on the 90s Blues Brothers American movie. Don't feel bad, I gave two thumbs up to the executive producer; not only did Psy seem to be a great addition to the talented cast, but thought that Lorne Michaels had finally caught up with the United States' demographic rapid changes and races diversity. Little did I know at the time, the South Korean rapper was already a sensation on social media with the official 'Gangnam Style' video racking millions of views on our beloved YouTube and registering a million downloads sold in just 51 days. Like bats flying out of a Dracula black cape, a myriad of the song versions started to pop up all over the world, even the Tango tempo wasn't exempt. In a short time, I came to realize that nowhere on this planet I could be safe from the 'Gangnam Style' infectious beats!

Right before I surrendered my rumba soul to Psy's demonic power as billions of Chinese did, please don't judge me, I stumbled upon a couple of folks, experts on South Korean culture, and some South Koreans on social media who were graceful enough to explain the subversive message of 'Gangnam Style'. Supposedly, beneath the bizarre dance and the video's absurdities, there was something to say about the South Korean society. To my surprise, 'Gangnam' is actually a real residential area in Seoul, the capital and largest city of South Korea. Described as a natural habitat of South Korea's super rich and trust-fund babies, it's a place of the most conspicuous consumption. There are also claims, long before the Chinese new aristocracy trend, South Korean 'Gangnam' residents have acquired an enthusiasm for facial mutilation and frequently visited hyper chic clinics, seeking a pointed noise, a jaw bone-cutting operation (ouch), and even rounded eyes. These coveted facial features are perceived as elegant Caucasian traits that one with money has to have.

The video was a mockery of people outside who pursued a dream to look like 'Gangnam' residents without the means to do so, and with no clue of what it really means, as a blogger well put it. It makes sense in environment full of disillusioned prey and vicious predators, an entire industry has flourished by supplying these wannabes a panoply of cheap and dangerous tricks and tools to self-bend facial features in the comfort of their own homes. I came across countless products guarantying a "Hollywood look". There are stories of teenagers putting on some devices that keep their eyes from blinking for hours, a cheap version of the double-eyelid surgery, and/or squeezing roller tools to get an oval form jaw line. Yet, these desperate juveniles' pain pales compared to a South Korean woman who was reported to have injected cooking oil into her face; she got disfigured beyond any surgical repair. Along these lines, in my view, the incomprehensible South Korean health policy-makers' muteness encourages these silly risks and life threatening trends.

I would be both racist and a hypocrite if I only put the spotlight solely on East Asian bourgeois and proletarians' appearance alteration addiction. The best sellers in my father-in-law's beauty supply shop, situated in a black American, Caribbean, and African populated district, have always been skin bleaching creams; he hardly keeps up with the huge demand of these toxic products. This trend simply reflects his customers' social class stratification based on a pathetic belief that black skin is inferior and that someone with a fair skin is more attractive. In 2014, almost two centuries after slavery was abolished, Dr. Keith Rowley's dark skin was cited as the only grounds of "objection" to his leading Trinidad and Tobago, a black country, as prime minister. All it would take for Dr. Keith Rowley to do is a dab or two of these radioactive gels on the body to peel the undesirable dark skin off like a snake to be entrusted with Trinidad's highest governmental position. Periodically, this process needs to be repeated to preserve the fake mulatto 'glow'. The most embarrassing fact and hilarious result is the uneven skin tone; but I quit laughing and almost pulled my chest hairs off (yes I have a couple) when I found out the active ingredients in gels that these apprentice dermatologists put on their skins. It is disturbing that you commonly find mercury (can damage the brain), hydroquinone (used to develop photographs), and arsenic (must sound poisonous, which is exactly what it is). Needless to say anything about black people perms and weave extensions infatuations. Although I myself have experienced a few peppery and blunt forms of racial slurs, I am quite unconvinced that my black skin and kinky hair were caused by some kind of birth defect or a malignant disease. And I don't think that my childhood hero and crowned King of Pop, Michael Jackson, would had swayed me otherwise.

The paradox, while other races are scheming to become white, Caucasians are racing in the opposite direction. The sight of pale people laying around like sloths under the punishing Florida sun used to spook me out until I was blown away by the overkill number of tanning salons around some of the Polar Regions of the United States. I am still haunted by French and Italian men bathed in baby oil and clad in thongs at the beach. And the energy that some white girls put out in gyms to reach their dreams of become a college vixen is quite impressive. I applaud their tenacity squatting it all out to get the natural black curves. As for the wealthy and lazy or aged ones there is an amalgam of dangerous plastic surgery options (lips, butt and breast silicone implants), that transforms any curvy challenged chick into *Sarah Baartman Hottentot Venus*. I see in my Caucasian male *compadres syndrome*, a Woody Allen hunt for the childlike physique of some Asian women (and men), an underpinned pedophile mania. I shall say that the risks taken by Caucasians to kick their whiteness down at least a couple notches are as life threatening as what other races do to become white.

There is no denying some indications that these cross-cultural mutilations are fuelled by racial prejudice. Yet, these awful trends could well be justified by our desire to acquire the splendor that the world chants ballads for. Let's assume this happens to be true, then these life threatening obsessions illuminate a couple of fundamental questions, if in a way, are people being caught up in spending to look rich, or are they simply chasing rainbows? Even further, I have been wondering if the term 'Globalization' is a cleverly adopted term to mask the self over indulgence which has been the western focal attribute and economic impulse. To a degree and taste, have we all gone 'Gangnam Style'?

"We no longer live life. We consume it."

Vicki Robin

After the irrefutable fact of sea levels and temperature records rising, prophets have been crawling out of the woodwork to alert the world of imminent disasters of biblical proportions. As scary as some of these predictions can be, the apocalypse can still be averted if we stop bickering and jointly get our act together. Then what does getting our act together really mean? The status-quo has been lucrative not only for big corporations but also for one special group; staged pedagogues are cashing in by formulating perceived factual arguments, which are nothing more than fictitious theories sending the world out on a wild goose chase or pitting one side against the other. In my view, the simple fact that we don't like change is holding us back from confronting the real issue head on. The root cause of our global headaches has been attributed to production, processing, and consumption. Yes, I agree that building factories create toxins in the process and the use of these products themselves not only creates pollutants and waste; but I cannot stress it enough, it also creates a taste.

Please be aware that some tastes have captured humans beyond the borderline of normal obsession and have brought empires down and pushed nations to the brink of collapse; the fall of the Tang dynasty is a cautionary tale. The Chinese Emperor Xuanzong neglected his duty, focusing on Consort Yang's insatiable appetite for lychees. I have a hard time to believe that big women were ever in style in China, but the Emperor favored her full-size build to the slimmer empress. Yang was known to gobble up excessive amounts of this exotic fruit daily. As a result, the emperor elaborated a superb system. Baskets of lychees were freshly packed from the southern region of China to be delivered to his palace in the capital by imperial couriers on fast horses, whose riders would take shifts day and night. And while Xuanzong was tending to his concubine's caprices, the rebel general An Lushan strengthened his army, declared himself emperor, and put the end to the Tang's mighty dynasty.

More recently, we were blown away beyond belief by South Korea's two-generation economic super jump that engendered their credit card addiction. Their astonishing growth made borrowing safe, but South Koreans didn't curb their appetite for borrowing after the 90s suddenly slowed economic growth. Even the government's solution to climb out of the Asian financial crisis at the time was cheering for private overspending. The same is to be said about a number of European countries such as Greece and Spain. These nations' crippling long history of borrowing landed them a few years ago, into the humiliating European Union's financial dog house, persistently mocked and bullied by Germany and England.

Then again, some other tastes have captured societies beyond the borderline of normal obsession, bringing some populations close to annihilation. It has been documented in the east of the New Zealand archipelago in the midst of the Pacific Ocean, the Maori almost exterminated their peaceful neighbor, the Moriori to control resources such as karaka berries. The story attests that isolated civilizations are not exempt from an outrageous greed.

Now that Bin Laden is assumed to be in the depths of the North Arabian Sea, you can well imagine an entire department in the Pentagon bored out of their minds trying to decipher the subverted messages in Shakira's hit song 'Hips Don't Lie'. How red their faces became when they realized that the song was, in fact, about the present-day threat to American children? This is the only way I could justify the United States, a warmonger nation, added a new front, the war on childhood obesity, to the list of wars it is currently entrenched in: the war on drugs, disobedient dictators, terrorism, piracy, poverty, illegal immigrants and legal immigrants, etcetera... Nancy Reagan was not content solely being the leader of the free world's *numero uno bunny*(a position Monica Lewinski would have killed to be elevated to), and her spirit of action landed more blacks behind bars than the total population of black slaves in the 19th century in America. Let's say Michele Obama, the first African American First Lady (and possibly the last) didn't feel it necessary to attempt reversing the incarceration trend set by her revered predecessor. Instead, she decided to spearhead the noble battle to save the future of the United States from junk foods. Yet, watching the line of overweight children running out of breath from the 2014 senseless shooting at Arapahoe High School and compare it to the 1999 massacre at Columbine High School, both in the state of Colorado where a lawmaker facing a possible recall election over her support for gun control resigned, put in doubt any of her claimed success!

We all know that any reputable business school insists on one directive to future gladiators. The only way for them to survive in the bloody competitive employment market is to make, by any means necessary, a lot money for their puppeteers. During my undergrad years, I sincerely considered tattooing the slogan on my forehead. The ultimate goal of a business is to see a simple taste of their products with the right blend of accessibility to plunge us into a psychedelic trance. Bottom line, the vision is to create consumers obsession

into a form of a dirty and taboo word, overconsumption.
Hold on! All the blame should not be put on these bands
of charlatans and psychopaths; as a consumer, this is the
ultimate perplexing instance which a larger number of
people from different races, socio-economic backgrounds,
and religious faiths all over the world have unanimously
decided to kill themselves together, resorting to mass
suicide rather than giving up their wants.

Let's start by openly addressing overconsumption.
Talking objectively about elements suffocating Mother
Earth and responsible for humanity's verge toward self-
annihilation without stressing the main factor, which is
overconsumption, is reprehensible; it is parallel to
writing about slavery without the critical role that Pope
Nicholas V played in 1452, triggering and vindicating
the organized global hunt for other human beings (of
other races and colors) by authorizing in a written
document to the King of Portugal to enslave any and all
non-believers in perpetuity! To digress for a moment,
although we reside now far away from the state of
Mississippi and Alabama, there is no way one could
describe how the 2013 British-American historical
drama film, 12 years a Slave, scared the hell out of my
slim, negroid bones. I don't have the speed of the
Jamaican sprinter Usain Bolt nor the endurance of the
Kenyan marathon runner Dennis Kimetto. I am an easy
target for Tippu Tip's descendants. The reason of my
concern is simple. To this day, the 1452 Papal order has
never been reversed!

Setting aside my nightmare, our avoidance of
chopping through our 'bullshit' is more that

overconsumption is much a part of our lives in modern society, and a habit vigorously sought after by third world countries. To change what has become the essence of our existence would require a massive global overhaul of our principles, not to mention the macabre economic prophesied wrecks. A drop in our cherished wasteful ways could be detrimental to the entire Bangladesh economy; morbid sweatshops all over Dhaka would have to close down. But don't worry. The end of our overconsumption 'swag' is not imaginable for any near future. I find reassurance that even the most remote villages on this planet have started to show signs of the global chronic pleasure; it has been way easy to find a bottle of Coca-Cola than fresh milk on any of the splendid hideouts I have explored. And I truly believe that it is just a matter of time before I run into a solar panel powered automated teller machine (ATM) in the middle of the Sahara desert, of course unscrupulously charging an arm and an eye for a transaction. I was once appeased by one of my 'oppressed' Palestinian friends while riding in his brand new german sports car, that our global emblematic slogan 'Veni, Vidi, Visa' will be chanted in harmony for generations to come.

"I know, up on top you are seeing great sights, but down here at the bottom we, too, should have rights."
                                                    Dr. Seuss

Before we got exorcised from our shamefully impulsive shopping habits, my wife and I went on a spending frenzy during Black Friday, the traditional shopping day after Thanksgiving in the United States. It was something we were looking forward to all year long. A few years ago, while we were reaping (or getting ripped off of) the fruits of our credit card debt limit increases, my gratification reached the pinnacle to find that most of the clothes strewn all over our living room floor, were made by the lovely people of Bangladesh. Having spent a small fortune, I wouldn't be surprised that we must have saved on our own the entire American retail industry and boosted the Bangladesh economy. Amongst countries I root for, Bangladesh had been on top of my list for a long time because of its people's sense of resilience. As in any bad divorce, Bangladesh's costly clash with the mighty Pakistan left it shockingly destitute. Although recently, from the nation's publicized economic boost and promising projections, at least what's displayed on extravagant spreadsheets, have given Bangladeshis a glimpse of hope to break from the addiction to foreign aid and international financial organizations inquisitions.

As I started to pay close attention after my initial assessment of Bangladesh's magical economic transformation, a string of horrifying information and images started to blow all over major broadcast news organizations and the social media. On November 30th 2012, I was alarmed to learn 110 Bangladeshi laborers were burned alive in a garment factory in Dhaka, the capital of Bangladesh. Not yet fully recovered from the shock, on December 1st 2012, 112 Bangladesh laborers were again burned alive in another Dhaka garment factory. And on December 14th 2013, it happened again. In all reported instances, some laborers were either scorched to death, killed by suffocation, the weak were trampled to death, and the desperately brave took the risk and hurled themselves from the few unobstructed windows to meet an often fatal, crushing death.

Bangladesh's slave-like factories have helped lift the nation to the top spot of garment exporters, trailing only behind the Chinese. The frequency of these crimes exposed the rampant corruption for the reluctance of the regulatory party to take concrete actions. Nevertheless, there are a lot bastards feeding this monster. Souls are still going up in flames, who should we send to the guillotine? On one side I see the aggressive, profit-margin obsessed supervisors. It has been reported that they ordered laborers back to their stations even as smoke filled up the air and alarms rung to the roof. But this group is no less evil than the authorities who shielded the greedy factory owners from any prosecutions, while intimidating, arresting, torturing, and even killing those who dare challenge their cruel practices. What about the person I see in the mirror? By shopping for rubbish in Walmart superstores now situated in every suburban corner, maxing up credit cards, and running over other rabid consumers on 'Black Friday' buying more crap and feeding this global phenomena of always trying to get more shit, I am sponsoring the immoral system. After a very short pause, I have reached a verdict. Due to the overwhelming evidence of neglect and selfishness, on the account of voluntary manslaughter, I found us, the consumer, guilty.

Although it is far from how I would cope with any sense of culpability, the Reverend Thomas Robert

Malthus, the first economic professor and coincidently my father's favorite economist (?), would have surely swung an iron bat a couple times at the Republic of Niger for its guts in trying to carve a share from the uranium exploitation on its soil by the parasitic French state-owned nuclear company, Areva. Any sane human being would find it outrageous that the company pays no export duties on uranium, no taxes on materials and equipment used in mining operations, and a royalty of just 5.5 percent on the uranium produced in Niger. One would also find it disgraceful that Areva's (which produced one fifth of the world's uranium in 2012) sobbing claim that a dime less from the bizarre benefits package will make its business in Niger unprofitable. The Republic of Niger reported a huge 7.5 percent of the world's uranium mining annual output compared to the country's disgraceful poverty is a paradoxical known fact. It is an abomination that around the world's second largest uranium mine one in four children under the age of five dies from hunger-related causes.

Then again, Malthus would have said that the famine in Niger has been a permanent cycle turning it into a reality, and children in this country must have gotten used to starving. What about poor France? The 1973 OPEC oil embargo forced this proud nation to embrace nuclear power to free itself from reliance on foreign oil. Unfortunately, this fatal move made Niger, one of its former colonies, once again crucial to its national interests. Yet the economic sacrosanct Pareto principle compels humanity not to take away the electrical power induced ease that has become

customary in France for the sake of saving lives in
Niger. If anyone in Niger would prefer to defy 'God's
will', the good Reverend Malthus would have suggested
they should quit procreating or pack up, walk through
the Sahara desert, deal with the Maghreb's subtle
racism in North Africa, take a good swim in the
Mediterranean Sea, and try to cross undetected, onto the
openly racist shores of Italy. What's in store for the
luckiest ones at the end of the rainbow who have
survived such a treacherous exodus? A life trapped in
the humiliating French romanticized ghettos, while
others will be shipped back, free of charge to their
godforsaken country, Niger. A couple of stubborn ones
will take on this journey again and again, until they
come to their senses and to the realization of their
destiny, life in Hell. As politely as Malthus clairvoyantly
stated: "In the lottery of life, the poor have drawn a
blank."

"The world is not going to end, but Mankind is stingy
enough to do any sorts of resets, that's why the world
resets itself once every while."

Chia A. Abdulkarim

Civilizations that have dominated the ancient western
world such as the Assyrian, Egyptian, Persian, Greek,
and Roman kingdoms, have all been consistent in their
barbarism and enslavement of other nations. To the New
World, Europeans brought with them industrialized
slavery, warfare, global distribution of alcohol, diseases,
and religion (black robes) concepts that destroyed the
Native North and South American cultural DNA and

environment. However, the most destructive was the effect of selfishness (individualism) and greed (Capitalism), combustible furies unknown to Native Americans at the time.

The existence of awful recorded accounts of fur traders gunning down 'savages' (Native Americans), including innocent women and children, sparing only *'Bois-Brûlés'* how it was widely accepted during that time. I still can't come to terms that scalping, the practice of removing the skin off the top of one's skull became a common ritual, was once in vogue; but in 1791 an enthusiast religious group offered a hundred dollars for every hostile Native American scalp as long as both ears were attached (Cleland, 1950). Alleluia, by the mid-1800s, changing fashions in Europe, manufacturers began to use silk instead of felt, brought about a collapse in fur prices and the end of the trade. Unscrupulous creatures like Jacob Astor has left undeniable marks on commerce practices as we know today, and his American Fur Company willed a miserable footprint to the current era's capitalists and corporations. Realizing that the mascot of my family alma mater, Florida State University, and the Redskins (American football team) fans were white dudes who painted their faces got me worried that the Native Americans' rescue never came on time in America. But cruising among the gambling palaces managed by Native American tribes, has brought on me a certain reassurance that the descendants of the few ones who were preserved and caged in reservations are doing way better than I am; or are they?

Another tragic account is the genocide (an estimated 2 to 15 million Congolese) in the 'Free Trade Congo' which is known to have financed King Leopold II of the tiny Belgium's quest for grandeur, building impressive public and private architectures in his Kingdom. Villages were required to meet quotas on rubber collections, and individuals' hands were cut off if they did not meet the requirements. Sadly, one who has toured the colonial Royal Museum for Central Africa could say that these claims are false and born out of my ingratitude toward Belgians and my twisted imagination; there is no mention of the atrocities committed in the Congo Free State, despite the museum's large collection of colonial objects. There shouldn't be any doubt in anyone's mind that, without the invention of synthetic rubber, mainly from petroleum by-products which, in turn, mushroomed lunatic Arab despots, the vicious Leopold II, and subsequently Belgium's as a whole violent colonization of Congo would have decimated my people. I am one of the direct beneficiaries of this frightening ingenuity.

The Congolese nightmare has kept on rolling even after the end of colonization. For more than a decade now, the Congolese's curse of having an abundance of coveted mineral deposits has flared the atrocity inflicted upon innocent men, women, and children to a genocide level once again (an estimated six million of Congolese dead and sill counting). Coltan (short for columbite–tantalite and known industrially as tantalite) is bankrolling regional despots' imperial aspirations. I am waiting for Silicon Valley to unveil this year's new gadgets and hoping once again that the world will soon develop an alternative way of making niobium and tantalum, used in electronic products, other than coltan, which will put an end to the current way of doing business.

As a confession, I felt seriously ill and disgusted about humanity as a whole while writing the first three chapters in this book because, at our base, we are all connected by our conscientiousness. Then I pulled an inspiring conversation I had with my father-in-law from my memories filling room in my dusty brain. Frustrated by his business and personal life's roller coaster ride, more downs than ups lately, he lashed out that the world is full of bad people. I couldn't help it but try to dilute his grim view of the world, and I said: "I'd like to believe that there is not a lot bad people on our planet, rather a lot of people who chose to do really bad things." Sadly, we have foregone satisfaction for gratification, 'Gangnam Style'.

V

False Prophesies

"Those who are really convinced that they have made progress in science would not demand freedom for the new views to continue side by side with the old, but the substitution of the new views for the old."

Vladimir Lenin

In early 2014, I let out the hyperactive child in me, sprinting in circles around our kitchen with my arms up like the great Muhammad Ali, raising my wife's suspicion that I got back on a drinking binge; I haven't, yet! I was simply overwhelmed by the news that the Dongria Kondh were able to knock out bully conglomeration giant Vedanta from disturbing the Niyamgiri hill for its rich bauxite reserves. The ruling in favor of the tribe provides a comforting level of justice, coming from a country where the 'Khap Panchayats', India's tribal courts, had ordered the gang-rape of a 20 year old Indian woman; a punishment for having a relationship with another Indian national but from a different community.

India's consistent contradictions are exhaustive to any passionate historian. Gazing at pictures of the

beautiful Taj Mahal, peace and serenity would find a
way in a serial killer heart. I shall confess that I do
respect India's appreciation for authentic body musk and
its cuisine asphyxiating odor; my faulty sensible nose
and a fear of an asthma attack have been keeping me
from traveling to this enchanted land and wander
around this gigantic mausoleum. India is a country
where a half-naked man asked politely the mighty
English conquistadores to get the hell out, and
surprisingly in 1947, they did. Then again, this nation's
past is as rich and stunning as its present. India's new
pile of rupees has helped this nation to launch a charm
offensive to the west to be seen as avant-garde. These
days, not only India has exponentially expanded its
service industry, it also hosts premiere research and
development centers of leaders in the high-tech trade.
The quantity and quality of patents granted in India
have caught up with the Silicon Valley in the United
States.

One of the most intriguing features of India's
culture is thousands of years of cultural transformation
infused with Hindu, Christian, Sikh, Buddhist, Islamic,
and other philosophical influences. On the surface,
Indians' sense of their great civilization's heritage seems
to have perfectly blended with the nations' chosen route
to development and prosperity, a bended form of
Capitalism. We all know well the unique capitalist
recipe for such a country with an inconceivable amount
of minerals deposits; "drill, baby, drill"! But dare scratch
the thin layer of the cultural lava, you get plopped with
a gooey curry scented mixture of disputes and
kleptomania that suck you into heroic Avatar like stories

that even prodigious screenwriters in Hollywood nor
Bollywood, could have outshined at penning a greater
epic ending.

For the Dongria Kondh, the Niyambiri hilltops is a
sacred mountain, the seat of their god that needs to be
preserved at any cost to maintain their livelihood. For
Vedanta, that same hilltop is Ali Baba's cave, a bauxite
mine that needs to be blast open by any means for Anil
Argawal's expansion. These too far-apart descriptions
and needs collided and ignited the fight. Vedanta's
fervent supporters were not only corrupt politicians as
well as a number of naïve tribe members who were
expecting a healthy share of wealth from the mining
project. These renegades were displaced from their
lands, and in return were given a bundle of shabby
concrete homes surrounded by barbed wire, laborious
mining work, a shack postured as a school for their
children, and a promise for more of these
blessings/insults. In the spirit of the same outrageous
scheme of preying on the innocent that Vedanta and
other conglomerates perpetuated directly or hiding
behind their subsidiaries (e.g. Konkola Copper mining in
Zambia) around the world, no indigenous people who
own the resources sought after, were ever given direct
shares of the lucrative project.

From our viewpoint, the Dongria Kondh are
relatively dirt poor and 'uncivilized'; they haven't been
invaded by mega shopping centers and automated teller
machines. Sadly, they have to resort to hunting for their
fresh meat and pluck free fresh produce from trees to
feed their families. As an analyst/bandit hired by

Vedanta put it, the Dongria Kondh are very poor on top with so much wealth under their feet. For this capitalist marksman, the only way to remediate this situation and reverse this picture is by destroying the ecosystem and excavate the rich ore.

As I glanced through the huge world map taped on our bedroom wall, my eyes zoomed to the Delta of Nigeria, where the same promise was once made. In this region, people haven't benefited from the oil drilling; rather, they experienced the poisoning of the waters and the destruction of vegetation and agricultural land by oil spills that pushed more indigenous into the abyss of extreme poverty; their depraved circumstances have sparked the delta's indigenous insurrections, seeking to damage the pipelines in a desperate act of anguish. This tactic executed by companies at its core, is not confined by racial motivations of superiority. I have been to Wales and toured the vestige of the English abuses and inhumane conditions surrounding the Welsh coal mining towns. Cardiff, the capital and largest city in Wales, was once the largest coal exporting port in the world; yet there are no traces of the wealth left around. As a result of my *tour du monde*, I applaud the devious Indian analyst ruthless pragmatism; yet the beautiful picture of the scenario he painted out never happened anywhere on this galaxy. It is a false prophesy.

"Globalization and free trade do spur economic growth, and they lead to lower prices on many goods."
Robert Reich

For centuries, there has been a big push for glamourizing globalization and free trade that stresses Capitalism's virtues; the efficiency with which prices carry information between consumers and producers, and allocate resources. Capitalist monks have come to take this theme as an article of faith, like gold. And if we follow Robert Reich, the leprechaun, on the other side of the rainbow, we will come to accept this utopia as true; I did!!! I have watched his documentary 'Inequality for all'. Sad catchy stories almost got me blind to the fact that he didn't bring anything new to the table, added nothing new under the boiling sun.

For quite some time now, I started to pretend to pay more attention to my diet. I became aware of my relationship with sugar was way off the charts. It is an addiction that spun out of control since I have moved to the United States. I was naïve to assume the abundance and relatively low price of sugar was due to production efficiency infused by technological changes. Little that I knew, through campaign contributions, Cuban brothers Alfonso and Jose Fanjul have gotten US congressmen on their short leash. Their success, according to government and independent studies, comes at a terrible cost to me, the consumer. I was dismayed to learn that sugar subsidies inflates The United States price of sugar, costing consumers about $2 billion annually in increased food prices.

What about people who live on the other side of the rainbow? Those are people where their governments want to increase minimum wage and analysts in the west caution and advise not to raise minimum with the excuse that it would make their countries less attractive to financial molesters, and less competitive in the Formula 1 cheaper labor Grand prix track. I would had advised these country's to forget raising the minimum wage for another reason; it is not a solution for inequality.

But even people on the other side of the rainbow do adhere to Nassau William Senior abstinence theory, built around the myth that people get rich because they don't spend. I am surprised that this pathetic excuse resonates across cultural and geographical boundaries. Looking around the world, Mukesh Ambani, owner of the one billion dollar residence, is not the first nor the only one kahuna who likes to flex their money muscles. What about Steve Jobs' magnificent boat he commissioned before his death to poke Russian oligarchs ego? What's to say about super expensive automakers like Bugatti and Rolls Royce who can't make enough cars to keep up with the ever increasing global demand? There is plenty of evidence dating back to edifices like the Egyptian pyramids and Roman orgies that crushes Senior's theory.

Fundamental questions about the morality of wealth accumulation has been long forgotten. The notion of greed is a virtue which leads to the explosion of blood sucking entrepreneurships. We are seeing the burgeoning of Free Trade Zones which are huge textile assembly plants near the docks that give a clear indication of the exploitative scheme sophistication and ampler. And for these modern economic molesters, it is vital for the free-economic-rape zones to be located around major seaports, international airports, and national frontiers. This approach gives them a tactical advantage; when laborers dare demand their right and protest against low wages and miserable working conditions, all the owners have to do is close the shops and relocate to another naïve third world country full of deceitful unpatriotic economists and leaders.

What globalization and free trade has successfully done is to force developed countries in over subsidized large sectors of their industries for national pride and to use their power in tipping the balance against other weak and obedient countries. And this kidnap-for-ransom scheme has been lucrative for their corrupt politicians. Sadly, the real side effect has been felt by the rest of the powerless world. The United States have mastered and won all the gold medals in this game. While our friend Robert Reich was serving as The United States secretary for labor and crusading for the increase of minimum wage, Bill Clinton was holding Jamaica by its throat while highly subsidized dairy companies from Arkansas, his home state, were squeezing and kicking Jamaican dairy sector's balls. In the documentary "Life and Debt" local produce farmers explain how potato, onion, and carrot imports from the United States have put them out of business, decimating entire villages.

Robert Reich was old enough to experience a pivotal consequence of Capitalism's domination and its most active tentacle, the democracy. His selective memory must have been erased at the height of AT&T's reign, the government sponsored autocratic monopoly over US telephone lines that lasted more than a century. In the name of Capitalism for a hundred and seven years, innovations in communication technology in The United States were held back because any invention that wasn't owned by the United States sole telephone service provider was banned and outside inventors were prohibited from testing their inventions. Testing any invention on the sophistically guarded phone lines was an odious crime severely punishable by a long federal prison sentence. And if you happen to live in rural areas or cities that the company deemed not profitable, oh well, you were just out of luck.

As a result of my *tour du* 'real' *monde*, I applaud the leprechaun's disturbing rationality and simplified conclusions; there is no gold at either the beginning or the end of this rainbow. It is a false prophesy.

> "Religion is what keeps the poor from murdering the rich."
>
> Napoleon Bonaparte

On February 25th 2014, I woke up to a news that I wouldn't imagine even in a million years; a despicable act of pure evil committed by black Africans on black Africans in a black African country. The Nigerian extremist Islamic group raided the Federal Government College in the town of Buni Yadi in Yobe state and massacred 59 little boys aged 11 to 18 as they slept. The corpses of some of these innocent children who had escaped with bullet wounds only to die from their injuries were found in a nearby bush land. For some reason, these lunatics spared the lives of young girls. These maniacs have set their eyes on anyone they deem "infidel'. Their list includes Islamic clerics, Muslim leaders, and political figures such as former military heads of state, Generals Muhammadu Buhari and Ibrahim Babangida.

Beyond their idea of creation of an Islamic state and other ridiculous demands, the essence of their grievance mirrors the anger of the disfranchised masses. Nigerians have had enough of unending scandals where the elite class are accused of siphoning billions in oil dollars out of the country's coffers and watching the elite class public displays of extravagance. Islam is not to blame for Nigeria current butcheries, the group Boko Haram (in Hausa means Western education is evil) has picked the baton from where Christian insurgent groups like the Niger Delta boys have left off but with obscene cruelty. As the gap between the poor and the rich in Africa's number one oil producing nation reach insanity levels, setting aside my emotions, it doesn't come as surprise that unemployment and hunger motivated young people to get over their fear of torture and imprisonment and to blindly embark on these crusades.

Napoleon Bonaparte had to know better; he rose from an institution whose sole purpose is to protect the nation's rich people interests. Armies have been traditionally used not only to conquer and rob other weaker or naïve countries but to squash the poor people who dare to demonstrate their dissatisfaction with the ruling class; and these days are no different. The claim that the fear of an invisible mighty creature keeps the poor from strangling the rich is as absurd as the most powerful pygmy dream to have the entire world at his feet. Once the consul of France, Napoleon's immediate push for reform of judicial code based on the new principles of equality of all before the law shows that he was well aware that prisons were built by elite to fill with the unfortunate. Even though the new code replaced contradictory regional codes and royal decrees, it didn't change the system in place that protected the rich and their wealth.

Shackles and other poor people in uniform are effective ways to keep poor people in line; but the best equipment in rich people's toolboxes is academia. Losing the sense of morality and shame, academic institutions have certainly been good to their generous benefactors. No other field has mastered in legitimizing social inequality from its conception as a science like economics. I found appalling that barter and the "dumb" trade which are some of the most egalitarian trade systems are the object of ridicule for today economic sorcerer's apprentices. These paid prize fighters have tricked us all to believe that throughout time a small group owns all means of production. Even great relativists like Karl Marx had fallen into that trap and eagerly broadcasted the outrageous fable. To his defense, he later tried to redeem himself by pulling the red carpet out from under capitalists' feet by questioning their origin. Nonetheless, this disheartening and reckless concept emasculate laborers. The truth needs to be told, but not now. But you will agree with me that the perpetual social imbalance is caused by a small group of villains who figured out how to control all other means of production and survival by the sword or mass manipulation. This goes for western spurred commerce systems adapted by the rest of the world; and today, the global consensus is that capitalists are well deserving to own it all, because they have been branded as "job creators".

Why do we fall in love with fools? I truly believe that anyone like Sir Paul Collier, who claims that colonization has nothing to do with the uninterrupted African mess that we witness today deserves the guillotine! And I swear that I am close to applying the Chinese water torture method on the next old stingy white lady that brings up the name of the confused Dambisa Felicia Moyo. I am disgusted that Dambisa's eminence and her African slave trade consulting expansion came at the cost of discrediting the work of incredible honest Africans and Non-Governmental Organizations that I have personally came across. Most people don't have much but have devoted their lives to lending a hand to the less fortunate. Aid is a transitional maneuver of relief for people stricken by Mother Nature's rage, and it works taken in this pure purpose and context. On the other side of the track, debt has worked for western country's to keep their economies afloat and to feed their nationals addictive spending. However, it has never been a catalyst for third world countries' development as intended for explicit reasons I cited in previous chapters. Certainly Dambisa, Collier, and the other buffoons appease white people's conscience and relieve them of a sense of guilt towards apathy. The devastating consequence of acceptance of their senseless stance, is the indication of the little we have learned of the social implications and danger from Joseph Goebbels' propaganda.

My wife, like many other suckers, rationalize that rich people's sporadic generosity is born from guilt. If she was right, such guilt would have made Bill Gates give away all of his fortune, shares in Microsoft, and with money in his bank account none of the Gates would have to live like a monk for generations to come; except he doesn't! The only coherent explanation, having tasted the good life on earth, the mere idea of prolonging the comfortable ride beyond death stimulates ruthless capitalist like John David Rockefeller, Andre Carnegie, and Patrice Motsepe as well as heartless monarchs and despots to kiss religious figures' rings, or after robbing the masses, to attempt buying their way out of hell through philanthropies. Religion is the only thing that keeps kleptomaniacs and tyrants from annihilating the poor.

Around the world, the crushing response to socio-economic inequality has been the sophistication of the lucrative incarceration system and the expansion of law enforcement. Throughout my travels, I found the same revolving door scheme that traps the non-threatening poor. No matter where I go and with a little effort, I can draw out a burning furnace that is fed by police nightly aggressive raids and sequestration of poor. Even after they're released, hefty fines tie them up in a court systems to generate fear and money to maintain the entire theme park. I empathize with Napoleon's

Corsican accent and poor grasp of French; yet claiming
that religion is what keeps the poor from murdering the
rich is his self-imposed misperception. It is a false
prophesy.

> "For every monarchy overthrown the sky becomes
> less brilliant, because it loses a star. A republic is
> ugliness set free."
>
> Anatole France

Let me be blunt, I disdain monarchy as a product of
brutal invasions and dark times, and even in its
capitalistic rejuvenated style, monarchies have lost their
relevance in the modern economic system. Why
rationalize granting a family and its small circle of
friends the full right of sponging off an entire
community? By blood line? The tourism argument skews
the monarchy's real impact; yes, the Japanese Emperor
attracts a lot of tourists that potentially generate
considerable revenue and economic activity. Yes
potentially; there are no facts to back this up, and the
staggering costs associated with maintaining the pony
shows orchestrated by their 'highnesses' at the cost of
their citizens pockets, appears more like a money trap
than a tourist attraction. Religion is often used to
vindicate the need of a monarch. Yet common sense
should prevail over this ridiculous pretext. Then again,
republics have their own kings and queens. Where
monarchs claim blood rights, political leaders, moguls,
and CEOs, just think they are better than all the rest
and should be compensated as such.

It's hard to stomach the remarkably above reproach perks of these esteemed 'super humans'. For depending on the eccentricity or depravity of their minds, these benefits range from mansions, exotic 'conference' trips, luxurious cars, and the power to the ravenous debauchery. "Umhlanga" is real! It takes place in the spring every year in the tiny nation of Swaziland during which the perverted King Mswati III gets to salivate on a parade of thousands of casually naked virgins, including his daughters, where he generally picks a new addition to his fleet of wives. However, it pales in comparison to Catherine the Great of Russia tales of regular intimate sessions with horses, when she ran out of willing suitors. And we wouldn't have known why the Spaniard King had racked up frequent flyer miles on African trips if he didn't break his hip and had to be flown back for emergency surgery. King Juan Carlos of Spain was pictured in front of a dead elephant with a riffle got the pink slip from Spain's World Wide Fund for Nature honorary presidential seat. The backwardness of the monarchy is in the power if its second layer, the aristocracy. I was baffled to learn that as modern as the English claim to be, its aristocracy still owns most of the land in Britain and retain ninety seats in the House of Lords.

There are also plenty of heads of state that are de facto monarchs. The long list of maniacs who have gripped the highest republic seat of power for more than twenty years includes Paul Biya of Cameroun, Mohamed Abdelaziz of Sahrawi Arab Democratic Republic, Alexander Lukashenko of Belarus, and Islam Karimov of Uzbekistan (majority of which are African head of state than any other continent). And following their steps and using the same tricks, there are a number of new Turks who have vouched to crush Paul Biya's record.

What can really go wrong when a head of state's appetite for grandeur seeps into their psyche? Take the village nut, Jean-Bédel Bokassa, a military officer who came to power after a coup d'état and after eleven years as president, decided to crown himself as emperor; following the steps of his idol Napoleon. The inauguration ceremony, which included a five million dollar diamond-encrusted crown, bankrupted the already impoverished nation. Three years later, France had to put an end of their puppet reign of terror mixed in Capitalisms' molasses after he ordered the massacre of schoolchildren who refused to wear uniforms made in a factory he owned.

I would concede that there are a bunch of ugly republics out there but worse things could be said about fat monarchs and paranoid monarchies. Moreover, a modern society's attempts at justifying a monarchy as symbolic to a nation's identity is pathetic. When you erase from the board every silly reason for a monarchy, what is left is the suggestion that nations with a self-imposed demeaning arrangement refuses to grow up. This explanation boils well with the late and almost last Tonga sovereign, Tāufaʻāhau Tupou IV, who claimed his servants are like children; they need a father figure to guide them. Conversely, what is there to say about a deviant father whose sole conviction is to perpetuate the long tradition of molesting his own kids? The reality of changing sentiments caught up with one, Gyanendra

Shah, the last King of Nepal. His misplaced assertions that he would never become irrelevant to his people were crushed and the monarchy abolished. What's to say of Aristotle's statement: "Monarchy is the one system of government where power is exercised for the good of all?" Sadly, it is an immoral prophesy!!

"Poor people are those who only work to try to keep an expensive lifestyle and always want more and more."
Jose Mujica

Historians lack consensus in determining the causal relationship between various events and the government economic policy in the Great Depression. For Keynesian economists, the recession was caused by the economic bubble. Monetarists believe that the Great Depression was caused by shrinking of the money supply. New classical macroeconomists have argued that various labor market policies imposed at the start caused the length and severity of the Great Depression. The Austrian school of economics accuses central banking decisions that led to mal investment. But I shall say that Marxian economists got the depression half way wrong, a symptom of the classism, and half way right, its instability inherent in the capitalist model.

However, there is a prevailing accusatory tone suggesting that the poor's greed led to an economic cataclysm like the 1929 Depression. Long disappeared from our minds, is Arthur William Cutten, who was one of America's most successful speculators and by the 1920s was one of richest Americans. But more importantly, he was the ringleader of consortiums which artificially boosted the stock market to an all-time high in the spring of 1929, leading to the Great Crash in October of that year. Have you heard the name Jesse Livermore, also known as the "Great Bear," and the "Wall Street Wonder," who was one of the most flamboyant and successful market speculators in the history of Wall Street? He was also one of the prominent speculators later blamed for having precipitated the Great Crash of 1929, during which he bragged in his book to have made over $100 million.

The 1929 Depression didn't happen because people were searching for employment and suddenly couldn't find it. I don't know if I should be appalled or amused when some suggests the depression was caused by the desire of the people to have certain salary expectations who chose to stay at home instead enslaving themselves for less. When any society disjoints its ethical safeguards, a group of wicked individuals will see a weasel hole to creep through and form cartels to distort the established symbioses for their gain. The pressure and veracity with which they pursue the gains, always leads to crisis raging from social to economical.

Now please, let's not play the ostrich game. The Great Depression of 1929 was not due to low money growth rates, labor resistance to take a pay cut and preference for leisure instead of working. Otherwise, the same is to be said about the German depression that led to the ascent of the nascent Nazi Party and Adolf Hitler in 1933. If it is true then, it should be true now. What is your verdict on the recent housing market bust? You and I have experienced the latest economic crisis that has

shaken the global faith in Capitalism. If you still believe
in current economists slogan, I am going to gently ask
you to remove your 3D glasses and humbly look at the
truth; crisis, ranging from social to economic, just like
civil wars, are manufactured or caused by cartels who
have overplayed their hand. And that is not a prophesy,
but reality!!!

"Every morning in Africa, a gazelle wakes up, it
knows it must outrun the fastest lion or it will be killed.
Every morning in Africa, a lion wakes up. It knows it
must run faster than the slowest gazelle, or it will
starve. It doesn't matter whether you're the lion or a
gazelle…when the sun comes up, you'd better be
running."
Christopher McDougall

There is something erotic about seeing a flock of people
enraged by the prominent flaws in Capitalism, which I
do agree are inequality and its consequential
discrimination. But like a forty year old virgin on a date,
I quit being hopeful when anyone addresses the cultural
deficiency of the currently dominant commerce system.
They constantly end up prescribing structural remedies,
which to me is illogical. When the people from the
'occupy wall street' movement in New York City were
asked how to resolve inequality, they slid down the
muddy pool of tax and democratic reforms, basically
maintaining the status-quo but demanding that
everybody get choked on their own vomit with the same
intensity. Such views are nonsense and dangerously
engraved into our minds by our inability or sluggishness

to contemplate an alternative commerce system, to derail from the irrational course, and to implement the obligatory cultural changes.

To twist Churchill's famous dictum, Capitalism is the worst form of economy, except for all those other forms that have been tried from time to time. While economists and wannabes are running around in circles with their thumps up, every morning in India, a woman wakes up and knows she must outrun the fastest armed bandit. In Greece, an immigrant wakes up and knows he must outrun the fastest nationalist. In Brazil, a teen in a favela wakes up and knows he must outrun the fastest corrupt police officer. In Chicago, a mother wakes up and knows her children must outrun the fastest gang members. In Russia, a human rights activist wakes up and knows she must outrun the tentacles of the cunningly swift agents of the kremlin. In Guatemala, a deportee lands and knows he needs to outrun a bullet. In Afghanistan, a polio vaccination worker knows she must outrun bullets the suspicious Taliban. Every morning in Florida a black teen wakes up, he knows he must outrun the fastest zealous armed white man. It doesn't matter whether you are a lion or a gazelle, when the sun comes up, they'd better start running or they will expire. And that is a real prophesy!

VI

Corruptibilis

"Travel is fatal to prejudice, bigotry, and narrow-mindedness, and many of our people need it sorely on these accounts. Broad, wholesome, charitable views of men and things cannot be acquired by vegetating in one little corner of the earth all one's lifetime."

Mark Twain

Tara and I are those friends on social media that tease our families, friends, and followers with photos of sunsets in highly desirable, and sometimes undesirable, locations on the other side of the world. It is our way of offering an opportunity to live vicariously through our experiences without costing our followers a dime. At first it amuses them, then promotes wanderlust; they have a little daydream about their next vacation and then the jealousy sinks in. Although I just made that generalization up, trust me, the disparaging comments and sly queries we have been asked would lead anyone to that conclusion.

People trying to find an excuse for carrying on with their morbidly boring lifestyle often asked how Tara and I are able to afford traveling to some of these amazing and unusual destinations. To my astonishment, I have been asked several times as a black couple, why we put our lives in danger crossing backwaters and driving through jungles at the mercy of cannibals; or simply put, do what is perceived as 'white people' foolishness! My answer to these cowards is that it's more than setting up a life of making a difference, the fear of never getting the essence of our existence is our driving force. And living a life of purpose and experiencing humanity's complexity requires getting out of the comfort zone and breaking taboos.

I shall confess that the heroic and romantic answer above covers up the true attempt of influencing the behavior of those around us, which I deem as a noble hidden agenda. There is no doubt in my mind, travelling is a life-shifting experience, the key to breaking that lazy and selfish way of thinking and the withdrawal from unhealthy mind-numbing routines. In economy as a science, the lack of connection to the human experience constructs a numbness that has landed economists into a poisonous pile-up. It is not surprising that 1st Baron Keynes who argued that the postulates of the classical theory are applicable to a special case. He then formulated and generalized a theory applicable to a special case. If he and other leading economists had travelled through humanity's darkness like us, meeting and conversing with the "savages" and not the savages disconnected owners, perhaps he would have foreseen the narrowness of his theory, and held back his eagerness of destroying David Ricardo's legacy to engage one of the most pressing issues of humanity; how to distribute wealth.

Then again, Keynes and his wave of contemporary economists have inherited the numbness and dumbness attitude from people like J.S. Mill who applauded Europe's most heinous creatures who took on the task of educating savage tribes, for the excuse that slavery was a mandatory stage for inducing them to work and making them useful to civilization and progress; while prior generations of mischievous political economists, who used their aristocrat connections and went at length to develop idealistic theories to strike down laws or attack a class that he didn't like. Power corrupt, brain power makes people corruptible!

"A wise man should consider that health is the greatest of human blessings, and learn how by his own thought to derive benefit from his illnesses."

Hippocrates

I've become accustomed with the cyanide smells of the struggle lingering in developing countries. I dance with grace on the upbeat tango of navigating between the aggressive limousines inhabited with the miserably elite and the loutish walking dead of the masses which reflects the bounteous of nations' social and economic butchering. However, the contrast between the civil servants worn out eyes I saw in Jomo Kenyatta International Airport in Nairobi, Kenya, and immigration officers arrogantly frightening demeanor in Maya-Maya, a flamboyant but vacant airport in Brazzaville Republic of the Congo, have shattered my paradigm. Right there, scientific evidence with jazzy graphs depicting the corruption index are not needed to crack open and decipher the enigmatic verses of corruption and corrupt practices. The two differing airports have left a clear impression that from one, you have left the developed countries' sphere, and awkwardly where embezzlement lands you in the big white house, the congress and presidency; while asking for "a little sugar" to the wrong person in another, places you in jail.

There is sufficient culpability to pass onto everyone. Even international experts, World Bank and IMF mercenaries, have ordered naïve and weak countries to put everything up for sale, privatize state-owned companies, while knowing well the dark thick cloud covering their states affairs, are fueling economic genocides. Nonetheless, it is imperative to distinguish the two cohabiting parasites, and in the case of third world countries, one is fatal and the other one has become necessary. There is the elite who are corrupt thieves whose paranoia of losing privileges and infatuation with western amenities and pampering, a lifestyle that has undoubtedly infected me, are crippling their nations. There are the circuits where very small amounts of illicit money and service are exchanged at a really fast rate, to amount to almost nothing at the end of the day. There you find the common people, angels with broken wings, who have become corruptible for survival.

I have participated in a conference where Peter Eigen was worshiped for his revered finger-wagging. He is quite a character who has managed to turn his once hobby while serving as a regional director for the World

Bank, into the roadshow of highlighting corruption and embarrassing governments that he ill-advised or screwed over. It is an outrage to pretend that third world countries dwarfed development is cause by civil servants, giving an excuse to hypocrite governments to prioritize short term economic fixes and squash informal entrepreneurs. To the defense of developed countries, it is indisputably a clever way of cleaning up the field and planting the décor for foreign multinationals financial wild masturbations and orgies. But I am not surprised, like my westerner's colleagues and friends, that Peter Eigen demonstrates the same sense of being out of touch with, or doesn't care about third country realism by lumping all together kleptocracy and poverty.

After repeated life threats, I have found that the easiest way in explaining my view of the difference between corruption and corruptibility and cooling off the public's penchant for adoring "white whales" is in making reference to our human body. On one hand, *corruption* is like *hookworms* which attack the wall of the small intestine and stunt the victim's growth and mental development. On the other, when people are paid meager wages, living in dehumanizing conditions, *corruptibility* becomes a way of sustenance. It is comparable to a *bifidobacteria* which is contained in the gut and exert a range of beneficial health effects, like the regulation of intestinal microbial homeostasis, the modulation of local and systemic immune responses, and the production of vitamins.

What are my advisable remedies to corruption and corruptibility in the current dominant sadist form of economy, Capitalism? I always argue that the wheel doesn't need to be reinvented here; from my experience working for the state of Florida in the United States of America, I can attest that the West already has an effective mechanism of hypnotization. If a system is scared to step away from Capitalism, the way to curb corruption is the baton, fair and equitable justice; and the sole cure to corruptibility is the carrot, investment in civil servants and set a minimum universal livable pay. Only then, it is relevant to a government to impose accountability and require integrity on it citizens. But these are two mild inconveniences of doing business in countries ruled by despots and political gangs.

> "For the powerful, crimes are those that others commit."
>
> Noam Chomsky

As a child, I was an avid reader of *Jeune Afrique* Magazine; more than any other article that truly captivated my attention was published right after the 1986 Philippine revolt sketching how Ferdinand Marcos plundered the Philippines of the wealth . Pictures of Imelda Marcos thousand pair shoe collection and racks of designer costumes encrusted with pearls left behind became to me the symbol of evil and greed. The French based journal never wavered to taking on controversial matters, exposing irresponsible leaders and their families' estates and shady deals. In response to the constant nagging, these powerful groups vehemently denied building up personal wealth through embezzlement, yet their assets were worth several times more than want these tyrants officially earned. The laughable spectacle has become extra colorful in the twenty-first century. Not only will a picture taken on cellular phone be instantly posted on Instagram, but freelance hackers have been driven by the hunger for scorning the rich and blowing the whistle on the powerful individuals and organizations.

Think about it for a moment. There is no way these twelfth grade level kleptocrats like ex-Zairean president Mobutu Sese Seko and their entourage of intellectual midgets, could have figured out on their own, how to ransack and sell state reserves of gold and diamonds, to pawn oil and timber lots, or to divert loans granted by foreign governments and international financial organizations. It would be careless to believe that the paranoid Saddam Hussein, busy strangling dissidents and gazing Kurds, had the sense and time to understand that instead of acquiring a high-end property in Venice, Italy in his name, he had to hide behind a Portuguese trust controlled by a Bahamian corporation that's run by a company registered in Lichtenstein!

Behind Capitalism's powerhouses' façade of righteousness, there are accommodating teams of well chic lawyers, accountants, bankers, and financial advisors operating from behind veils of secrecy provided by legal customized loopholes. The stream of fortune funneled out of damaged nations would never have succeeded without these masters of deception. The world financial centers maintain that these legal loopholes are only one of many indications these capital migrations are government sponsored. As an illustration, to preserve the "Françafrique" silly dogma, French state prosecutors blocked every legal procedure against their "former" colonies living tyrants.

Okay, now you should be asking yourself why these western sanctified nations are quick to starve any disobedient states like Sudan and Iran of investment whereas do little to stop sitting dictators and families from renting their financial drawers to stash their ill-begotten fortunes? First, it provides a large flow of capital for their economies. Most importantly, this blood money often receives special red carpet treatment until these bungling morons lose their firm grip on their starving citizens and generally get booted out by a more desirable replacement. Western country's decisions to freeze assets belonging to Zine El Abidine Ben Ali and Muhammad Hosni El Sayed Mubarak after they were ousted by the Arab Spring deluge smacks hypocrisy because they knowingly and willingly helped these tyrants hoard gold bars and acquire vast number of 'diversified' assets.

Just to name a few, what has happened to the spoils of Haile Selassie, Saddam Hussein, Somoza of Nicaragua, the Salinas brothers of Mexico? If a lesson has to be learned from Sani Abacha's case, the short flamboyant Nigerian military dictator general who died of a heart attack while under an Indian prostitute, it is not a happy sequel. It has taken Nigeria years of court battles with embezzlement hubs and using, ironically, teams of well chic lawyers, accountants, bankers, and financial advisors operating from behind veils of secrecy provided by legal customized loopholes to recover a small fraction of the several billion dollars fortune that Abacha and his family amassed by misappropriating public funds during his six year rule. In other cases, after carving out the legal fees for tracking a dictator's money trail, countries are surprisingly presented with lint and excuses.

Despots grooming and attending to their fortune is a lucrative business for western countries and now Dubai is putting on fierce competition. I am not amused by universal blames and accusations of looting nations coffers loaded solely on mentally retarded leaders and their cronies while the real masterminds and conspirators behind these Houdini acts enjoy freedom and go on to have a long and prosperous but unethical livelihoods. Western schemers have to turn a scrutinizing eye on themselves and be held individually responsible and face justice for these crimes against humanity. Tough sanctions need to be imposed on countries harboring theses financial poachers. Only then it will be right for rich countries to impose accountability and require integrity on the troubled nations.

Interlude III

It's funny how my emotions led to complication

My tears has yet to change the situation

My temper doesn't resolve the equation

People want an explanation to our creation

Every kiss champions the crème of my devotion

Humanity lost the foundation to a unique aspiration

It is crazy that everything we do has already been done

Yesterday daring dream is just gone

Our world is hanging on a sample bone

Millions of souls are raging for the throne

Even our common desire comes at a different tone!

Mind diving in the past to feel like a newborn

Gorgeous angels feel like exempt

Should break their wings and repent

Tears going down my dry face like a serpent

Anger should be banish to the full extent

It is sad how no matter life thinks love grow

Time always persuade cupid to leave the show

Real joy is cover with a skeptic blow

When sensitive mind try to make body stay

Spontaneous soul walks away

It is scary how the judgment day will be brutal

Innocent opinion will be vital

Looking up the pretty sky will be fatal

Like diving in the book of great fire

Expectations are rolling like a flat tire

Why should Lucifer be hired?

Trying to sway a heart so fat

Avoiding evil to plug in a rat

Good fortune might make you cry

Perfect love might pass you by

But nothing prevent you to try

Break down the chain and fly

Are you going to be stopping by

And just to whisper 'Hi'

Then suddenly goodbye?

This poem is dedicated to all of the "Mohamed Bouazizis"
and revolts

VII

Mohamed Bouazizi

"Poverty is the parent of revolution and crime."

Aristotle

Paranoia is said to be a categorical symptom of schizophrenia but Edward Snowden, the former United States National Security Agency analyst's lullaby has exonerated people like me and vindicated my "I fit the criteria and qualifications of a Mr. Nobody"; at this point of the book, having ridden and survived the intense waves of my rants, would now approve that I am well deserving of at least two dedicated spies keeping their eyes on me twenty-four hours around the clock. And in case you are one of the analysts who would be tasked to painfully decode the odyssey of my thick, black foggy skies of my emotions, I shall now attempt to ease your assignment.

Everything burgeons out from the comical contradictions in my life. I am an obnoxious and introverted socialite. I occasionally organize a banquet and invite friends and nemeses to my home. After the meal, I am quick to see everyone leave because I feel exasperated by the long intrusions in my tranquil abode, unless the gathering turns into a cerebral ultimate fighting championship. Not for lack of discernment, I am shameless to declare that I have perfected the art of pinpointing the hot button topic that will ignite an emotional thunderstorm out of my guests. The more heated the debate, the more my appetite ensues towards victory. Nothing clutches my attention nor sharpens my viewpoints more than an intellectual scuffle with oral strokes. Indeed, a number of these bloody battles and insults have been transliterated from madness to conversable in this book.

There is another crucial aspect of my life. One of the best pieces of advice I ever received, had come from a Nigerian politician who I took to a strip club at an 'undisclosed' location in The United States He was caught in his birthday suit in the *boom boom* room. When I swore to him no one would ever know about this incident, he replied: "Always air out your dirty laundry before your enemies do."

The older I get, celebrating and waiting for death to make its inevitable appearance becomes monotonous. I have long purged myself of daredevil antics and fruitless affiliations. Long gone are the days of using my body as a testing ground for experiencing psychedelic drugs to assuage the hauntings of my childhood. Long faded is my enthusiasm for getting pissy drunk and christening my backyard, overlooking the glittering nightscape into dawn. Family and friends have only high praises for my adopted healthy and dull lifestyle. And yet, I have a secret that will break more than one heart. The media's voluptuous coverage of banalities and the relentless

assault of hysterically delivered facts based on pundits'
personal opinions added to my penchant of sparking
heated debates. I admit it, I have found a new vice. Yes,
I have become a news junky! I could not have had better
timing.

The recent rapid increase in accessibility of
incredible technological developments including "smart"
televisions, TiVo, smartphones, and high speed internet
connections have lessened barriers of time and distance
to allow addicts like myself to indulge in our insatiable
cravings for information and entertainment even within
the comfort of our cozy bed. These days, I could walk into
a McDonald's restaurant in The United States and
stream live the beheading of a zeta member by a rival
drug cartel in Juarez Mexico, write and record a cheery
narco corridor gangsta song inspired but this tragic
event on my laptop, buy a gun from a pawnshop and
make a music video in my bedroom posing naked with
my neighbor Bangladeshi's pit-bull, sell millions of
copies on iTunes, get paid for every hit my video gets on
YouTube, and pay off my hefty student loans. And while
I am building the mental strength necessary to be
infamous and effortlessly rich, the Arab
metamorphosing chronicle has been quenching my thirst
for extreme dramas.

If a television station could crank out an award
ceremony for the Arab Spring debacle, I am more than
certain that the most melodramatic collapse of all Arab
caliphs wouldn't go to that of Yemen's half-baked former
president, Ali Abdullah Saleh; hands down, the award
would be bestowed on the former Libyan leader,

Muammar al-Gaddafi. The colonel's rambling rage on
Libyan state television left folks from Tokyo to the
middle of Wichita, Kansas dumbfounded. For the
majority of us who have gotten the sour taste of tyranny
and were brought up under an institution of deifying a
paranoid schizophrenic leader, Gaddafi's antics rightly
met our expectations. I never anticipated such a clown
who overcame the western *shime-waza* and played with
fire for so long to end up as a bleeding ragdoll,
videotaped it all his pitiful glory. It is clear to me now
the *Africa's King of Kings* committed two cardinal sins:
The zealous threat of killing Libyan dissidents like
cockroaches and of divulging generous contributions
made to French and English leaders whose armies were
slowing down his butchering. It didn't help that a legion
of capitalist gougers were waiting at bait for the colonel's
ungainly descent to get their grimy hands on Libyan oil
deposits.

   Gaddafi's infatuation with texting and checking his
'likes' on Facebook helped big brother to locate his
foxhole. The upset posturing of Nicholas Sarkozy and
Tony Blair led them to spare no time in smoking Gaddafi
out and tossing him to the incensed citizens of Libya.
More than the humiliating death of African's King of
Kings, I was disappointed by the stand taken by Saif,
Gaddafi's son. His Ph.D. thesis at the enshrined London
School of Economics was entitled *The role of civil society
in the democratization of global governance institutions:
from 'soft power' to collective decision-making*, but his
rhetoric substantiated that the thirst for power trumps
common sense. The kid was as crackbrained and
heartless as his father. *tel père, tel fils!*

With the activation of the Arab Spring, I watched in bewilderment, young disenchanted Arabs confronting brutal policy and government hired thugs, flocking strategic centers of their cities. On paper, Arab countries have made extraordinary jumps indicated by the eradication of polio and rise of Gross Domestic Product. This is an attractive but incoherent story. In reality, the honey pot has been wasted and disproportionally distributed. Still standing are astute and filthy rich U.S. sponsored monarchs such as the embattled maniac, Russia and Iran's protégé, Bashir Assad, who has been shaken like never before. All of the remaining Arab's autocrat puppets positioned by the west, have since tumbled like a house of cards.

The development of the events from the Arab Spring led me to speculate that the illiterate but ardent youth around the world in the 1950s who took heroic steps demanding autonomy and dignity must have mirrored the exhilarating and foolish optimism as today's tech savvy but naïve Arab kids in the midst of the revolt. The same faux pas made during the call for countries independence and civil right furies in the last century has been replicated by the Arab Spring this century. The bloodshed for freedom in the 1960s halted national public humiliation. Regrettably, their young leaders' gullibility bought time for colonization's metamorphosis. As nations' independences were spoiled by morons, former colonial powers orchestrated their version of the '*Night of the Long Knives*' that kick started in Africa with the coup d'état in Togo in 1963 and replicated a domino effect everywhere else. The successful plot is epitomized by France's unrelenting socio-economic molestation of its 'former' colonies in Africa and the Caribbean with unabashed impunity. A pathologic abuser should never be left in the same room supervised or unsupervised, with any everlasting adolescent country. At its core, if a fledging nation is not given time and insulation from outside interference, its ability to articulate a collective and pragmatic vision for economic development is stunted and leads to economic turmoil. Indeed, passion is not a substitute for vision!!!

As the social explosion dragged on, divided groups emerged with differing and obscured agendas which shadowed the upright central purpose of combating economic disparity. The rising chaos became the perfect breeding ground for extremists groups, a new breed of villains. The Libyan televised civilian carnage hasn't evolved into the expected pretty picture conceived in Benghazi while the city was under siege by Gaddafi's death squads. In the media, the complex narrative of demand for dignity and for fair distribution of national wealth was reframed and reduced to a context that western tele spectators can grasp, the cliché word, democracy.

The sobering number of lives lost and people displaced since the beginning of the Arab fury have broken my enchantment for pundits' constant bickering on television. I should be celebrating for overcoming my addiction for desensitized news. Alas, the mental clearness has crippled my soul under the weight of unbearable consciousness. The painful realization of disintegrating memories of the young Arab whose despair and humiliation pushed him to set himself on fire, triggered a general sense of indignation: "Mohamed Bouazizi."

"A little rebellion is a good thing."

Thomas Jefferson

Even though change is certainly inevitable, common mortals don't have the nerve to take destiny in their hands and tip the outcome in their favor. Homo-sapiens' indolence explains slavery, tyranny, as well as our ovation for outliers. Indeed, I applaud the rejuvenated 'rat pack' of defiant nations that are creating a new myth. BRIC is an acronym used in a Goldman Sachs report from 2003, stitching together economic roaring powerhouses Brazil, Russia, India, and China. South Africa, the mulatto token in the group, was added later on. There are superb colorful graphs and charts that ornament what all the fuss is about. Digging and retracing these nations blueprint ascent is of extreme concern.

China survived Mao Zedong's unfathomably vicious cycle of trial and error, and error, and error, and deaths which was the nation's amazing great leap backward. Then you have to respect the man of his stature and power admitting his experiments plunged the country into famine and poverty. Russia endured political and economic chaos, the long walk of shame after Mikhail Gorbachev threw the towel in the cold war ring. Not surprisingly, he has since been crowned the most hated man in Russia, whose false news of his death triggered waves of celebration all around the macho nation. How did these two goliaths *endogenous* growth scheme pull themselves out of the Communism and socialism Dark Ages, resuscitated their prestige, and added a Wladziu Valentine Liberace glamour to their mix? Easy, they became their brother's keeper. They didn't shy away from the dirty little word, protectionism.

For Brazil and India, it is a tale of two countries. These two nations who lacked the muscle and stubbornness to confront their benefactors, are the real reasons they had mastered the exogenous growth method. In Brazil, Father Lula da Silva's majestic serenade that galvanized the vultures and hypnotized prey was instrumental to a once called *Belindia*, and a la Franklin D. Roosevelt, launched infrastructure projects. The same goes in India; for Narasimha Rao's pragmatism was helpful to navigate through the biggest scourged democracy. However, history hasn't been kind to the "father" of Indian economic reforms. While Lula has been sanctified and paraded around the world, Rao was at the end of his life humiliated and forgotten. It should be noted that the rise of Brazil and India is from their respective romantic tales of beating the odds. How did they up their economic status? These nations didn't bother to reinvent the wheel. They are simply doing what was done to them before; diligent self-colonization. This commercial and trade model taps into the vast potential of these countries rampant and streamlined corruptions systems.

As I continue divulging my list of trespasses, I once fervently cheered Brazil's comeback move from the comfy honeymoon with the WWII Nazis and a long tradition of dictatorship. It does help that Brazil's export of soybeans to China has surpassed a staggering five billion USD. Alas, the needs of mammoth soy farmers like Cargill, a multinational company which controls the majority of the soya bean trade in Brazil, have been used to validate the deforestation of the Amazon forest and the brutal expulsion of its indigenous population. Brazil is now the world's fourth largest consumer of nutrients used in fertilizer and herbicide production, behind China, India, and the United States. Despite this fact, the application of the product to crops is still low in comparison to countries with more developed agriculture; in recent years, a noticeable increase in the rate of children with cancer and birth defects in the population of the small time farmers living around these big pharm agro domains is in correlation to the increased exposure to a variety of Monsanto's potions sprayed on the land. And it doesn't take a genius to figure out why the Brazilian government doesn't bother to take any action.

One could suggest that the global epidemic of incomprehensible human abuses is necessary on the premise that something has to give in order to get; or in Brazil's case, something needs to be taken by force in order to prosper. A few years ago, Brazil was dethroned as the most skewed nation in the world, and I can see it will be gaining the prestigious crown back in few years to come. I have observed Brazil's particular out of control appetite for China's yens like crack cocaine to an addict. Like any long-time drug abuser, at some point, the obsession induced by chasing the dragon of extreme euphoria, they will engage in illegal activities, even sell out their own children, to support their habit; and that is what Brazil has been essentially doing to keep up with their economic growth.

The BRICS have shown symptoms that signal the next stage of commercial and trade maturation, and the normal progression cycle is world domination. China's Lenovo has been digesting IBM's PC business and cheap Chinese copies of luxurious goods that now extend to cars are giving traditional players a run for their money. Indian generic drug makers are taking full advantage of the legality of copying brand-name drugs whose patents have expired and, in turn, inundate the pharmaceutical world market. Brazil's rapid internationalization process catapulted their soy bean producers (Mato Grosso) to the top. While Russia's oligarchs obedient to the Kremlin have been collecting the professional sport teams and players around the globe.

For any nation keen to step in the second global economic division, it is impossible to replicate the BRICS chess moves due to the complex realities and advantages of individual countries in the pot. Contrary to purported fantasy, the BRICS nations did not think outside the box; they mounted a little rebellion and dared to look inside the box. The miracle claims are as real as Santa Claus or Pope Jean Paul II's sainthood. Evidence points out that these countries basically cranked up their engines and caught up with their destinies. When I am asked to explain the BRICS emergence my answer is: "Brazil got back on the saddle, Russia outlawed clowning, India found its way back to the race track, and China taught the dragon how to count!" What about

South Africa? "Oh well, it cut the deal with Lucifer and surfed its dying waves." Amen!

"The wolf always charges the lamb with muddying the stream."

Elihu Root

Our parents' horrible divorce combined with our father's newly found political stardom, threw our family's social contract into chaos and sprung my sister Betty's reign of terror. As the sanctified state of Israel and the canonized Rwanda, my sister Betty figured out that she could use her petite stature and everyone's guilt to get away with terrible evil deeds. Once she mastered her malicious scheme and could hypnotize the man at her will, no one was exempted from her shake down. I am right now shaking as I am reliving those childhood memories; yet my childhood fear is not comparable to children in Rwanda forcedly recruited and sent to the battlefront in DRC or angry children in Palestine facing heavily armed Israeli soldiers. Betty's cries hit supersonic high notes that rung in our father's ears hundreds of miles away and derailed anything he was doing; and like possessed by Lucifer himself or Lilith, the man would drive franticly across town and busy streets of Kinshasa the same way the United States urgently dispatches its mighty forces in the middle east to protect its interest. The man rolled the head of anyone she pointed out.

Like the spoiled brat state of Israel, there was no sharing; Betty wanted it all and got it all. Anyone who dared challenge the legality of her supremacy over the entire house, faced bogus accusation of threatening her life, liberty, and happiness. On little or no grounds, the suspicion of threatening her was enough to earn this black rose retribution. Betty would have the right to kick and punch the condemned person and any conspirator who were forced to stand still until she quenched her thirst for blood. Eventually, our dad had enough of the terror and put the end to her caprice, partially fearing for his own life. The fool, power drunk, turned against Maximillian Robespierre!

Instabilities manufactured around the globe have recently received a backlash from the western public. People living in these hades on earth have partially to thank the media for streaming traumatizing pictures of innocent children being butchered. Peace had to be imposed on the sub-Saharan Africa region; in the same line, the world is now learning to disassociate denunciation of Israel's massacre of Palestinians in Gaza from anti-Semitics and is considering legitimate criticism of Israeli policies such as the condemnation of the inhumane blockade of Gaza. And Hamas has long become more of a business than angry extremist group calling for the end of Israel. One could naively believe that these two revolutions have something to with wisdom, an eye for an eye leaves everyone blind, or their obedience to their master when ordered to yield. Rather it is in the spirit of Capitalism, these overzealous bullying actions added a wave of economic shakiness felt around the globe.

"The end may justify the means as long as there is
something that justifies the end."

Leon Trotsky

Long before I was taken by a semi-Haitian woman who I
ended up marrying, Haiti was to me a destination
engraved on my bucket list. I was enthralled by
everything the half of this Caribbean island came to
project. It is an ecstatic emotional mishmash of the
romantic song 'Haiti Cherie', with heroic stories of naked
black savages with bones through their noses triumphed
over the mighty Napoleon army, and the Haiti
nationalistic anthem 'union fait la force'. I shall confess,
learning that the international airport Toussaint
L'Ouverture wasn't equipped with a control tower
dented a bit my enthusiasm. After the earthquake that
upended the shitty spot of Port au Prince upside down,
billions of donors' dollars were reportedly poured into
the country. I couldn't wait to be amazed by the number
of infrastructures built as a result, and that notion took
precedence over the fear of planes colliding in the air.
Then again, I discovered that the Haitian tourism and
business industry has long since died, and only a
negligible number of airplanes land on the tarmac daily.
In the spirit of true conquistadores, my wife and I took
on the challenge of crossing this lost paradise from south
to north with our rental car. At the end, the expedition
was far from what I envisioned, extreme on both ends of
spectrum of elation and regret.

For anyone who has ventured beyond the
demarcation line drawn around Port au Prince and the

fortified monkey cage of Labadee, they would agree with me that the rest of Haiti is full of magnificent sceneries. The view on top of the Citadelle Laferrière created by Henry Christophe, a dive in the blue water of Bassin Zim near Hinche, and a pilgrimage to the epicenter of Haitian *voodoo*, Sau-d'Eau, blew my mind away as divine and soothing. The human encounters while driving through the inside corridor of route nationale 3 and the coastal highway of route nationale 1, is unique to anywhere we have traveled to before. Moreover, there is more to taste than to write about the brilliance of its seafood and cuisine. Haitians would go on and on to recite tales of their extraordinary washed-out apogee, and more than often, folks flanked us with stories which were no more than morose bragging rights of the past. Is it really impressive among those who perished on the Titanic that there was a Haitian passenger on board?

I for one cannot comprehend how churches are the only trusted banks, issuing treasury bills redeemable at full value afterlife and get away with this scheme for so long. The imposing presence of churches at the center of every city, town, and village was a clear indication of rampant misery. There is no doubt that prolonged poverty and desperation cripples a person to turn to betting on life after death. Nonetheless for Haiti, Christianity shouldn't be the gateway religion of preference. There is no way to disentangle voodoo from Haiti's history of booting out the French and Christianity from slavery and atrocities committed by France on this part of the island. In my eyes, Haitians' embarrassment and denunciation of *Voodoo* deities *Loa, Congo,* and *Parrain Ogou,* and they embrace of

Christianity is a vicious punch to their heroic ancestors and legacy.

Before embarking, I paused to reflect on the journey. This half of a tiny island with its provinces equally dramatically poor and fueled with regional egotistic antagonisms is a lack of *bon sens* and no sense of urgency melting pot. As I piled historic layers of Haitian socio-economic disintegration, I found a country where a minority comprised of Petion's grandchildren, mulattoes, Lebanese, and Syrian Jewish immigrants, have formed a mafia and controlled with despicable arrogance every lucrative industry in Haiti. Regrettably, the Haitian Negroes' lack of common sense had spoiled our tour and the diaspora can't help but bleach their skins and then lament about the state of affairs was nauseating. I came to the same conclusion as one of my Haitian friends. What had happened in Haiti wasn't a revolution. Rather, it was a successful slave insurrection instigated by mulattoes, who strived to capitalize on the romantic anger of the revolution to grab every seat of power.

In a country where a Jamaican voodoo priest *Dutty Boukman*, convinced ill prepared slaves of their invincibility and immortality; outnumbered, they confronted and defeated the sadistic Napoleon army. Over two centuries later, facing a socio-economic pandemonium, there is not a droplet of the equivalent life-force anywhere on this heaven packed with shadowy seraphs. Throughout history of this prideful nation, Haitian heroes have been foreigners. One could conclude this nation's salvation would have to come at the hand of a non-native. Alas, there is Bill Clinton, Thomas

Jefferson's progeny. Clinton for one is not Boukman, but rather a true *financial boogeyman*. It is with shame and agony that I say Haiti's degradation has no end in sight.

The moon orbits around earth and the earth orbits around the sun. All Arab Spring revolts have turned into a big fiasco. They have successfully raised the consciousness of a broad mass of people but the inadequacy of the Arabs Spring is in the clashes of the goals and political positions of movements squeezed under a noble umbrella. Mohammed Bouazizi didn't torch himself because he was refused a right to vote; rather, he was asking for economic freedom. Throughout the twentieth century, spikes of blind fury had similar consequences. Lumumba was sickened, revolted, and was tortured to death. Ernesto Che Guevara got fed up, revolted, and was blasted into little pieces. Steve Biko got pissed, revolted, and was gunned down. Salvador Allende couldn't take it any longer, revolted, and was bombed in the presidential palace. None of the narratives of these heroic figures had a favorable outcome. Unlike Gaspar Yanga, they ignored that revolt shines bright like the sun but *there is no revolution without landing on the moon, a place way cooler than the sun!*

VIII

Say Whaaat?!!

"Climb mountains to see lowlands."
Chinese wisdom

You may hear the voice of the speaker, but not whom he echoes, and that is the real danger. After another dreadfully long economic class, I made a pit stop over at my good friend's apartment to refuel my soul and blow off some steam. To avoid him trying to sue me, we will call him 'Jerome'. He was in his usual temporary deactivated mode, high as a kite. The relationship between Jerome and I brings me back to my catholic boarding school years. To skip the obligatory siesta, I hopped in the confessional box where a half asleep priest would pretend to listen and to care about my little lies and shenanigans. Poor 'Jerome', I must have worn out his buzz by lamenting the entire evening how erroneous the chauvinist Nigerian lecturer was and how the rest of the academia pin fundamental principles and in this case, arbitrarily knock off Jean-Baptiste Say and hang Thomas Robert Malthus using John Maynard Keynes animosity toward their fame. *Nonetheless, all three happen to correctly describe what the symbiosis of*

*the market was during each respective time. It is
irrational to expect the same deduction from people
living during different transitional stages of commerce
and trade maturation.* I even used the velocity of
circulation of money in my closing argument to simplify
my rage. I hold as truth, at the exception of slavery and
cannibalism, that verity exists in relation to historical
context. I don't know if Jerome was surprised or
shocked, but all I heard coming out his mouth was; "Say
Whaaat?!!"

Thanks to the battle royal between Thomas Piketty
and the Financial Times (*please disregard Piketty's
childish solution to the most complex plight of our
existence),* to my and others' delight, economic disparity
was pulled out from the trash bin and became an
erogenous topic for the moment. Unfortunately, it turned
out in an *elitist cockfighting.* For my generation, it
sounds farfetched there was a time when bestial greed
was frowned upon, and very few would believe that
adulated philosophers, Plato, Aristotle, Cato, and Cicero,
saw charging interest on loan as a crime. Sanctioning
European monarchies who then controlled and looted
the entire world, in its heydays, the Catholic Church
decreed anyone who engaged in usury couldn't receive
the sacraments. Going ten steps further, Edward I of
England passed the *Statute of Jewry* that made usury
illegal and a blasphemy. Well, these restrictions and
threats turned out to become a gold mine for a group of
usual bandits. You have the Hebrew speaking peoples,
who circumvented biblical prohibition by charging
interest on to non-Jews and paid dearly later on for their

sins, and goldsmiths who figured out to exploit the public trust and profit from gold placed in their safe.

I have come to believe in the existence of a villain gene that is overly active in business titans and serial killers, while that same gene lies dormant in the rest of us. You have to be more than a modest douchebag to send your children and your lovely wife to one of the most ridiculously poorest nation on earth, Burundi, to spend days staring at the family struggling to carve out a dignified life. After your family experienced third hand poverty, snap them out of it and jet them back to the wealthiest country in the world where they reside in one of the most luxurious and high tech mansions known to humankind, while leaving behind the Burundian's family to their melancholy. When your backyard is more fascinating than Jurassic park, I guess touring Disney world is boring!

On the other hand, Bill Gates' senseless act didn't open the floodgates of hell. There are plentiful accounts of such acute indifference around the globe and throughout time. Pope Francis is famous for teasing the dispossessed. The absolute Sovereign of the Vatican City State invites the homeless to share a meal in his sumptuous palace and quietly send them on their way back to the streets. Going back to the Roman Empire, by the end, the rich went after lands of indebted peasants who took up loans to keep up with the out of control tax demands. And when I travel overseas, I am chagrined by the meager pay that my well off family members, friends, and acquaintances hand to their dedicated and hardworking servants. These subtle and not so subtle

acts of inhumanity only project the image of the general
wickedness, and I myself in this chapter, attempt to
explain how we fell neck-deep into the nth abyss. We
have never been able to fully pull ourselves out of it,
instead, we have resolved to keep a great number of us
behind enemy lines!

"Do not look where you fell, but where you slipped."
African wisdom

The economic field has been knighted for its *alleged aim
to make humanoid pecuniary quotidian better.* This
regarded noble art have been gangrened by its infancy
missteps. The dark side has piled a considerable number
of sandbags that has sustained avalanches of realism
and equality. Case in point, the deflection of David
Ricardo's deduction on profit by celebrated lecturers who
choose *to ignore contextual facts and instead denigrate
the importance of this classical economist's depiction of
profit relative to his epoch.* These felons defiantly
disappear and give a standing ovation to Ricardo's
impulses and aberrations when it adds to their personal
mystic. Ricardo's stinging crusade against the
landowners were not for naught; nonetheless, his
classification of profit is vindicated by later events.

The Napoleonic Wars added fuel to the *Corn Law's*
fire and provided the chaotic front to skew the price of
grain in England artificially high. At the end of France's
fruitless war that crushed their superpower standing,
corn prices plummeted in England and as a result, the
entire English economy took a nosedive. Alas, the brunt
of the damage was felt the most by the laboring class. At

the beginning of the 19th century, labor laborers'
livelihoods deteriorated from cash payment and an
occasional meal on the landowner's table, to meager
social services doled out by the parish under England's
Old Poor Law. The miserable harvest of 1828-29 ignited
riots and sabotage by laborers who resented the
unfettered landowners' greed. Deplorable but
indispensable chaos of such magnitude are a breeding
for ideological gun slingers. As today's economic
academia is jam-packed with pranksters, the 19th
century was a crucial time for an art that would come to
reign supreme over commerce and trade, was no
different. Seems like the same soul transposed onto a
different body. At the disjuncture of common sense and
scholarly opportunism, there were individuals who saw
themselves as fervent guardians of Capitalism; and in
England, the mecca for economists, *Nassau Senior* was
one of the most skillful and coldhearted of the group.

When elephants fight, it's the grass that suffers. For
somebody who has survived a dictatorial undergraduate
orthodox institution and is now fighting off nips from
zombies in one of the few remaining heterox graduate
programs in The United States, I shall attest that the
heckling from both sides has left me virtually brain
dead. Unexpectedly, during a lecture on Abstinence
theory and the man behind it, Nassau Senior's discourse
by one of the last standing Marxists, *Fred Moseley*,
awakened my inquisitiveness. I suddenly realized
crucial historic moments and unusual characters
underwriting the main trade and industry creeds, have
been lost in the long folklore of sham bickering between

the economic sacrosanct trinity of Adam Smith, David Ricardo, and Karl Marx's unrepentant disciples and their antagonist's neo-classical gladiators' offspring.

As I embarked in the "folly" of getting acquainted with Nassau Senior and his abstinence theory version, the lack of proper approach and dissection of Senior's assessments and intrigues almost dampened my enthusiasm. Not only there exists a limited number of literature on Senior, but they center largely on the proverbial tango in fighting between Senior and his contemporaries, which I am going to ignore in this chapter, and the decisive role he played in the triumph of evangelical political economy on the 1834 Poor Law Amendment Act in the United Kingdom. Yet, to understand Senior's ideological leanings, one must delve into the man himself. Obviously unable to get the face to face time, since Senior died a little over two centuries ago, I plunged into his published work and examined the influential mentors he associated himself with and the relationships he fostered in his career.

The socio narrative underlying Senior's Abstinence theory makes it necessary to put into context the United Kingdom's economic climate and intellectual dogma clashes during Senior's era. Divergence of a valid frame for wealth distribution was, and still is, at the core of political economic clashes. Nonetheless, Senior's boldness molded the consensus on the rationale of wealth creation, tipping the balance in favor of capitalists. It would be a disgrace not to shed a light on Senior and the people that have influenced his opinions. Even so, Senior's Abstinence theory's core contentions are on the origin of capital and why we pay interest.

Furthermore, I hope that from Senior's critics and cheerleaders' assertions and reflections on the Abstinence theory's affirmations that transcend geographic and cultural boundaries, will revitalize more than a disillusioned prospective economist's appetite for this discipline.

"One lives in the hope of becoming a memory."
Antonio Porchia

In the previous chapters, I painted the décor of critical events that are engulfing my generation and threatening our future existence, and permitted the apogee of a fallacy that has come to be the silent socio-economic foundation of our time. With a drumroll, now it's time to meet the originator of a concept poisoning our ability to sail to the right shore, the Abstinence theory, which is the prevailing consensus on capital and interest of our time.

Nassau Senior was born on September 26, 1790 in Compton Berkshire, England. Senior's insolent analysis of socio-economic rifts of his era, could be traced back to his privileged upbringing. One could only imagine his life as the eldest son of the vicar of Drumford in Wiltshire, the Reverend John Raven Senior, and of the solicitor-general of Barbados' daughter, Mary Duke. His marriage to the famous English adventurer's daughter, John Mair, was the least ordinary. Then again, Senior was not totally insulated from rampant poverty. Having spent his early age in his father's country parish and combined with his father's role in his community, he undoubtedly observed the slow agony of the labor laborers and the impenitent ascendance of the landowners, his neighbors of course. The well recorded English worker's decaying condition shows that around the time Nassau Senior was five years old, a worker received three and a half loaves of bread as means of subsistence. By the time he was 27 years old, the meager pay shrank to two loaves of bread. He might not know a lot about inflation, but he sure could recognize the face of a hungry man.

It would be a great mistake to conclude that Senior's blitz assaults on the poor and protection of the wealthy have solely to do with his pedigree. The young Senior went to attend Eton College and Magdalen College in Oxford. While there, Senior's most important encounter happened after failing his first exam attempts. His search for a private tutor landed him into the hands of a quintessential and provocative figure, *Richard Whately*, who indoctrinated him to the *Oriel Noetic tradition of combining natural theology with political economy*. Whately inflexibly believed in the necessity of integrating morality and theology in economic analysis to draw 'correct' policies.

Senior did earn a law degree in 1815, but his problems with public speaking stood in his way of a long and fruitful career in the conveyancing field. I suspect, the fact that he found economics more exciting than law made him lazy to overcome his handicap. Senior abandoned his conveyancing aspirations and immersed himself successfully in political economy. He became *the first Drummond professor of political economy at Oxford* in 1825, and subsequently went back to this position two

more terms in his lifetime. During Senior's first five year
term at Drummond, he wrote an analysis of economic
definitions, published as an appendix to his now
comrade Whatley's Elements of Logic in 1826. He later
published a number of his lectures such as *Economic
analysis methodology* (1827*), The theory of money and
international trade* (1830) and *Population and wages*
(1829, 1830). Once he gained respect and acclamation
from the contemporary political economists, he never
looked back towards his initial lackluster career.

With his Whig party friends coming to power in
1830, Senior's sphere of influence exponentially
broadened in strategic areas of the United Kingdom.
Sadly, Senior was an Oriel prodigal operative rather
than a philosophical radical portrayed by some. He and
his Oriel Noetic counterparts seized every opportunity to
alter English socio-economic fibers and to propagate
their agendas. Senior became a key member of several
commissions: the Poor Law Inquiry Commission in 1833;
the Commission on Factory Conditions in 1837 and the
Commission on the Distress of the Hand-loom Weavers
in 1841. Senior proposed that the Amendment of the
Poor Law act aligned with the Noetics' agenda and
attested his unwavering loyalty to his mentor Whately.
The New Poor Law act was basically pulled straight
from John Davison's consideration of the Poor Laws
(1817) which proposed abolishing relief to the "able-
bodied". They naively rationalized that the vulnerable
populations such as the sick, elderly and children would
be looked after out of public funds in places like
charitable houses, orphanages and hospitals.

Alas, Senior's manipulation of English economic and
political policies went beyond the Whig party reign. He
advised successive British governments on trade, wages
and education issues. He assaulted with a verbal iron
bat, the macabre Malthusian theory of population
growth. To the great satisfaction of his puppeteer
Whately, Senior blasted Ricardo's feeble theory on rent
because it suggested a class conflict between the
landlord and everyone else; it denied the harmonious
laissez faire utopia and the existence of divine wisdom.
In the later years of his life, he spent his time roaming
around the world, and from those travel experiences
brought forth analysis in the form of journals that he
kept in Turkey and Greece (1859) and subsequent
conversations and journals in Egypt and Malta (1882).

Senior died in Kensington, London on June 4, 1864, at
the age of 74.

It is noteworthy to point out that as the legitimacy of
capital accumulation and interest was beginning to be
revisited and questioned, pious abstinence notions and
other alterations on the same premise from other
economic druids were orated throughout Europe around
the same time. Outside of England, we have the German
Max Wirth, the Swiss Antoine-Elisee Cherbuliez, French
Bastiat, Josef Garnier, and more attention is due to
Germain Garnier, who could actually be the first daring
sage to lay down the apologetic justification for capital
accumulation and interest. Even though they were all
pathetic, Nassau Senior's Abstinence theory was
crowned the original, and going against any logic,

became subliminally an integral part of English capital theory and today's social class's negotiations and concessions. Indeed, it is the white elephant in every recompense "negotiations" and table discussions.

"That every person is desirous to obtain, with as little sacrifice as possible, as much as possible of the articles of wealth."

Nassau Senior

The highly natural impulse, at first, is to delve into the modus operandi behind Senior's concept which has been a point of contention by many academics. Senior himself tried to cover his tracks by justifying his rage against 'an arrogant laboring class, resorting to strikes, violence, and combinations' for the reason that it was to him 'a threat to the foundation not merely of wealth but of existence itself'. It is suggested that his basis was a wrathful impulsive reaction to laborers violent attacks against whom he perceived as the vulnerable Capitalism profiteers and guardians of humanity's rightful order. It may be an unworthy suspicion to Senior's defense, but he initially published the Abstinence theory as the Outline of the *Science of Political Economy* (1836) a few years after the peak of laborers strikes and riots in 1830. Yet factual evidence put his sincerity into doubt. During his first term at Oxford and a couple of years before the Swing riots, the second lecture of the second course he taught (1827-1828) was on his Abstinence theory.

Most frequently, the term *abstinence* has come to be defined as a "psychological mechanism of repression

referring to sex, alcohol, or food". I even came across a
website suggesting parents should teach their fat kids
that abstinence is "a person's ability to delay
gratification relates to their ability to recognize the
rewards of patience and waiting, while at the same time
being able to practice impulse control, self-control,
willpower and self-regulation." I am sure that is not
going to work; it is no match for the scheming tactics of
the junk food industry and their marketing teams'
seductive campaigns that shrewdly stalk the kids from
vending machines in schools and are attached to every
superhero they emulate. The same reasoning goes for
adults; the pseudo human inaptitude to refrain our
desire is actually fuelling the booming financial advisor
industry. Therefore, a support to Nassau Senior's
assertion that it takes a certain individual strength and
sense of sacrifice to accumulate wealth.

Nassau Senior's Abstinence theory is by far his most
obscene betrayal to political economy. Awkwardly, this
slogan has been widely embraced and chanted by
demagogues and apostles who have adopted the laissez
faire as a divine law.

Setting aside all the finer details, the essence of
Senior's Abstinence theory of capital formation is a tale
of heroic abstinence from consumption that enables
saving to create capital. There is a dramatic depiction of
industrial capitalist's sacrifices in a guise to loan the
financially reckless labor laborers their means of
production. Senior's explanation clearly overstretched
Smith's motor of growth theory, which is saving. Alas,
Senior has managed to gather a consensus in the
discipline around the Noetic's belief in the wealth-virtue

symbiosis, a conviction that men of wealth, as to say
industrial capitalists, needed to be morally supported
and the beneficent divine order had to be fiercely
preserved.

Alfred Marshall brought to economic philosophy a
fascination for barracudas looking for ways to
demonstrate their mathematical and puzzle-solving
prowess that unfortunately comes at the expense of real
life studies. But no other concept exposed Marshall's
frailty in the development of the theory as the
explanation of capital accumulation did. And so, there is
little to say about Marshall's criticism or contribution to
Senior's Abstinence theory. If nothing else, he did
acrobatically replace the term 'sacrifice' for 'waiting'.
Nonetheless, Marshall was the critical step in the
process of toning down and polishing Senior's blunt and
uncouth concept forward.

Where Marshall's contribution to the capital
accumulation debate is blurry, it is very clear that
Böhm-Bawerk decided to tiptoe in, out, and around it. In
Böhm-Bawerk's acclaimed study of treatments of
interest, he took on Senior's Abstinence theory and
suggested that "Senior's doctrine has been judged much
too harshly." It is in his belief "there is a core of truth" in
the concept and there is no denying that capital
accumulation "does demand an abstinence from or
postponement of gratification of the moment." Then he
derailed from the assumed trajectory by pointing out
Senior's "logical blunder to represent the renunciation or
postponement of gratification or abstinence, as a second
independent sacrifice in addition to the labor sacrificed

in production." He goes so far as demonstrating that capital accumulation, like labor, is not a sacrifice, rather an alternate choice that one makes.

Then again Böhm-Bawerk 's bloody cockfighting with the ghost of Karl Marx rendered his explanation of capital accumulation not satisfying; he was adamant that somebody needed to save out of income earned to get the *necessities* for laborers to produce more output of higher quality. To keep an eye on the ball and not confuse means and ends, more attention is due to certain aspects of Böhm-Bawerk's analysis as he was anxiously plugging in his beloved time preference concept on interest.

I take a pass on another of Senior's principles on capital accumulation partisans; as eloquent some were and effective on the spread of the Abstinence theory, I deem their contributions as putting lipstick on a really ugly pig.

"Dogs don't rationalize. They don't hold anything against a person. They don't see the outside of a human but the inside of a human."

Cesar Millan 'The Dog Whisperer'

At this point, I have to look across the horizon to find a rebellious voice in *Ferdinand Lassalle*. Lassalle successfully made a mockery of Senior's theory by calling the Rothschilds as the chief "abstainers" in Europe. Actually, the Rothschilds were amongst the European vultures who exacerbated the discord and hostility between the North and the South. During the American civil war, these financiers reaped huge profits by working both sides of the street, as usual. But the man himself, LaSalle, was an effective socialist operative that provided an interesting parallel to Nassau Senior. Louis Blanc's view of social problems, poverty and economic crisis, underlined Lassalle's political scheme as Whately's view on Nassau Senior. And like Senior during his time in the United Kingdom, Lassalle was in relations with the most prominent of German minds; he had ample means and influential friends. However, Ferdinand Lassalle foolishly challenged to duel concurrently with a Bavarian diplomat who forced his daughter to renounce Lassalle and to Count von Racowitza. As a result, he was mortally wounded at the age of 39.

Another worthy challenger of Senior's Abstinence theory is *Isaak Illich Rubin*. He rebuked Senior's scheme as it was based on a mental superiority of "industrious and farsighted people" and blasted it as "being useless as an explanation of economic phenomena." For Rubin that "the Abstinence theory falsely" didn't explain how "Capitalism came into being and the basic features of this economic system." The doctrine wouldn't pass the litmus test even in a primitive state of commerce and trade in a country. To sum everything up, Rubin dismissed Senior as 'what one might call the economic barrister of the English factory owners'.

Rubin's personal life tragedy is an irony of bad taste. Rubin was first arrested a year after he published History and Economic Analysis (1929), and was accused of being a member of the All-Union Bureau of

Mensheviks. After being emotionally and physically broken, he was released on a commuted sentence in 1934 and allowed to work as an economic planner. Rubin was arrested once more during the Great Purge in 1937 to never be seen alive again. After all this was not in the hands of industrial capitalists, rather the class he so defended, labor revolutionists.

I find a good deal of justification for Lassalle's potential of shattering Senior's Abstinence theory on capital accumulation, though indeed the same is true for Rubin. Regrettably, Lassalle's premature death and Rubin's tragic demise cut short the chance of galvanizing a dialectic counter offensive. And so goes on the consequence of Senior's Abstinence theory on capital to mold the impending ideas on interest.

"Greed is all right, by the way I think greed is healthy. You can be greedy and still feel good about yourself."

Ivan F. Boesky

The nineteenth century English laborer worker revolts elevated the question of capital and interest into a social problem. Yet a detailed examination of the link between capital accumulation and interest is unnecessary once lured into Senior's Abstinence theory's premise of sacrifice. Simply put, interest is the reward earned for the "pain" of relinquishing money to the borrower. Senior's description of interest as a return to abstinence was another blunt delusion and yet, became the deep-rooted foundation of mainstream economic theory. Judging by the impact of his analysis of capital and interest on the theoretical economic field, Senior has more far-reaching implications than the prevalent classical economists, Smith, Malthus, and Ricardo.

Eugen von Böhm-Bawerk insisted that the value of future goods diminishes as the length of time necessary for their completion increases not because it is spoiling in your refrigerator. Furthermore, there would always be a difference in value between present goods and future goods because people are dumb and careless.

Alfred Fisher, one of the founders of the Race Betterment Foundation that advocated racial segregation for "preservation of the human race", a major center of the new eugenics movement in America, went further than Böhm-Bawerk 'perspective undervaluation of the future'. Fisher called interest "an index of a community's preference for a dollar of present [income] over a dollar of future income." For him, interest is the cost of one's "impatience" which creates a holy "opportunity" for another to take advantage of it. I sure would have liked to see his face when he lost a large part of his wealth in the stock market crash of 1929, and still thought that the economy would undergo a quick recovery.

Push forward to today's world, usury is now justified as a risk premium taken by capitalists. For George Riesman, it is the cost of the emotional roller coaster one will undergo for letting people hold onto their money. It is like a game show participant who may choose one of two doors, one that hides $100,000 and one that hides $0. Regardless of what it is behind the door the contestant is guaranteed $10,000. But for some reason, the laboring class doesn't get to enjoy the same

treatment; George Riesman doesn't advocate for the
laborers to get paid any premium for the risk taken to
show up to work.

George Reisman and the like are allowed to flourish
in an environment where people are more obsessed with
pulling more verses from the sky on price 'stickiness',
fantasizing about an 'Aryan economic' being, than
making reality based economic inquiry; and
unfortunately, the more abstract and irrelevant
economics becomes, closing the door to discussions on
critical questions that originated the entire discipline on
capital accumulation and interest. Since no one has
loudly been objecting to Senior's fairytale, it's the
assumption that there is unanimous acceptance, isn't it?
Speak now or forever hold your peace?

> "The distance between insanity and genius is
> measured only by success."
>
> Bruce Feirstein

The American's Abstinence theory was largely
influenced by the 18th century Swiss physician
publication *l'Onanisme*. In this treatise, Samuel Auguste
Andre David Tissot asserted that masturbation causes
"a perceptible reduction of strength, or memory, and
even of reason" that opened the body to a number of
diseases like gout. Due to the fact experimental trials in
the science were practically nonexistent and long before
society came to learn about testosterone, people took it
at faith that every sperm is sacred.

More than a century later, in the United States,
reverend Graham made Tissot's divergence theory his

Trojan horse. The good reverend believed that people needed to abstain from red meat because it increased sexual desire and therefore advocated a diet rich in nuts. He waged a battle against masturbation, as he deemed, was weakening the fiber of the society. But Graham's theory flopped, as he ran out of venues to disseminate his sermon and was chased out of cities by butchers. His successor, Dr. John Harvey Kellogg came at the time when sentiments towards Graham's notions had changed and he was held in high esteem as a hero and genius. He even upped the ante and promulgated that women shouldn't masturbate either. He then provided a tool for parents on detecting if their children were masturbating. As a deterrent to this vice, he outlined astonishing punishments: Men and boys should have their foreskin sewn shut with silver wire or circumcised without anesthesia; women and girls should have their clitorises burned with carbolic acid. As Kellogg's ideas were embraced with no resistance, he set on developing an anti-masturbation food. Yes, it turns out that our beloved snacks and breakfast cereal customs are supposed anti-masturbation foods!

I went at length to compress the twist in the American sexual probe in the goal of drawing a disturbing clear parallel between Tissot's divergence theory and Senior's Abstinence theory; they are both scripted from what the originators saw as humanity's imperfections and drew about reprehensibly erroneous deductions. While the former has been shattered by the work of Alfred Kinsey, the latter will still have a firm grip on economic theories.

"His hands would plait the priest's guts, if he had no
rope, to strangle kings."

Denis Diderot

Economy runs on selective memories and its ability to
accept absurdity. I had once a microeconomic course
where the professor flat-out confessed that nothing we
were going to learn in his class was facts based and
based on incoherent assumptions. Then he lacked any
intellectual integrity by throwing us hardballs exams. I
must make another weird confession. My childhood
mentors have ingrained in me, the idea that westerners'
frugality has made their world better than ours, the
Democratic Republic of Congo. Even on my travels
around the globe, I encountered the same lame
justification expressed from the poorest downtrodden.
When American billionaire David Siegel was asked why
he wanted to build the biggest house in America, his
answer was simple: "because I can!"

My pretend to be rich diversion is going on a $100
shopping spree at TJ Maxx. Of course, I am shocked that
someone can get a handcrafted diamond and rose gold
pacifier for $136,000, or pay easily $290,000 for one
romantic night in a submarine. In 2001, American
businessman Dennis Tito shelled out a reported $20
million for his 8 days in space. Not counting the private
jet industry booming in Nigeria, Russian oligarchs'
shopping spree of celebrated professional sport teams to
add to their collection of yachts, and the fact that
luxurious automobile makers that are worth more than

a million dollars can't make enough to meet their dough-lined clientele's demand.

Rejecting the existing God but believe in the existence of a higher power excludes you from claiming to be an atheist. We tend to ignore, as political power tips the balance between upper economic classes and openly keeping labor away from the dining table (attacks on labor unions), the predatory skills and ability harnessed by one, is the sole qualification and partiality of getting rich. Since humanitarian guardians like Pope Francis I and current economists cowardly retreat or are silenced from posing the moral question on capital accumulation, it should not come as a surprise to anyone, under the current applied premise, Senior's proposition. Any approach such as increasing minimum wage would be roughly setting back the clock on social economic disparities with the same consequential result and nothing other than Capitalism's self-preserving answer to inequality. Capitalists will gain it all again. We come to confuse verity to popularity; we neglect factual truth in place and embrace unrealistic assumptions. At this point, any reader who adheres to Nassau Senior's parody, this is the part where you have to get the hell out; run for your life! I would sincerely advise you to close this book and burn it. Otherwise, the rest of the marathon will be unbearable to your tarnished conscience.

As I was typing the last line of this chapter, I decided to return my old friend 'Jerome's' call, a sign that I was alive and kicking. There was rumor around my long absence, was a result of my wife tying an even shorter leash around my neck, which is moderately true, but I let him know I was busy writing a book and will be making reference to him in this chapter. I don't know if Jerome understood what I said or was afraid that I will be blasting our Pandora's box wide open, but all I heard shouted out on this other side of the phone was: "Say Whaaat!?!"

Interlude IV

Are you scared to explore such an area
full of expertise and only existing
to be pleasure for others, causes one
to quiver with delight but to
be apprehensive as well
letting go of all thoughts and just
exploring the heights that can
only be imagined to reach is
a burst full of greatness in itself
to shake uncontrollably and
release sounds that are only bought
upon by the highest high is the
solution and the problem
once such a feeling is experienced
one can only hope to reach beyond
again and again, wishing to find the
level of high to which one can never come down

IX

D.R.I.P.

"Like all great travelers, I have seen more than I
remember and remember more than I have seen."
Benjamin Disraeli

I long fantasized that one day, I would be writing
this chapter. Congratulations readers! You have
made it to the midpoint. However, I had no idea how
exhausted I would be after the incessant highbrow
foreplays and violent cerebral orgasms. The
contradictive twins of good and evil both dwell in me,
and this emotive convalescence has thrown down the
gauntlet, forcing them to aim at the same goal and play
nice to make sense of the global mess we are engulfed in.
If the electrical *conscienceversion* did smoke out the
remaining neurons you have left, I bet that you are
ready for the next stage of rational chemotherapy where
you might be pulling out your own hair instead of letting
the poison do it for you. Thus far, my hero is you the
reader, for your persistence, stepping over the dead
corpses of Capitalism's carnage, and magnificently
emerging undeterred, out of this labyrinth. For the
confused and emotionally weary who have forgotten how

we got here, let me recap this expedition before I tie you
on a raft and push you down the rapids.

Right off the bat, I shared with you an agonizing
encounter with the real face of inequality and one of the
many haunting pictures of socio-economic miscarriages
that rape my conscience day and night. The particular
personal tone in the letter addressed to Mama Vincent is
a concern for her sufferings and misfortunes born out of
the recognition that this sort of tragedy could have been
my reality if my parents' nasty divorce and subsequent
custody battle landed me in my illiterate and vagabond
mother's hands instead of my egotistical and callous
father's jurisdiction.

After the mea culpa, I tipped my hat to my unusual
muses and colorful instigators of this puzzling quest to
revive the world we all live in and unlike my cowardly
contemporaries, to gut out genuine answers as well.
There is no doubt, without every one of these individuals
and events, this book would have been a disastrous
boring date that you and I are on. Yes I said a date; I am
a bi-curious writer. That is to say my words and spasms
don't discriminated against anyone.

I sure hope that you understood Kamikaze was not a
tribute to the young Japanese men's crazy sense of duty
that demoted the humanity in them. Rather, this
chapter quizzes your awareness of poverty and the poor
who are a group that so many people are quick to judge
and to abuse. Have you realized how a lot has been
debated and how little proper actions have been taken to
eradicate poverty? Do I see poor people? Yes I do, and
you should if you haven't.

Craving of wanting more of everything that Karl Marx and Thorstein Veblen decrypted pales in comparison to the global twenty first century consumerism. This insatiable life-force has been wrongly attached to westerners with their ambiguous religious faith and barbarism and has been mistaken for the poor mimicking the rich. China, Greece, and I, stand as testimony that hedonism is one of the million flaws common mortals and societies are laced with. The devil in all of us wears Prada and holds a Kalashnikov 47. The world has gone crazy, Gangnam style.

I started putting money aside to build Paul Krugman's shrine in my office after I read his blog *New Thinking and Old books* until I realized he received a Nobel Prize for his feeblest jab; instead of lamenting about the obvious, why doesn't Krugman bring forth a pleasing new fragrance to economics putrid droppings? His tribute to *Capitalism in the 21st century* demonstrated that the global yearning for a messiah blinds even the most cogent of economists to the extent that he prophesied the book could be "the most important economics book of the decade." This witty man and confirmed paranoid guardian of Capitalism, mistook seductive 'noises' for the real signal. This book could have also dedicated hundreds of pages on false prophecies, but many before me have beaten this dead horse into the ground. I for one, am not a fan of fanning the propaganda of Capitalism's illusory spectacle.

I once believed that the justice system is not kind to accomplices, even if they take no part in the actual crime. Lady Justice has always been depicted as

blindfolded and holding a balance scale on one hand,
representing impartial discernment. I have come to
realize that her tiny scale cannot possibly weigh the
white-collar wrongdoings of most of the financial thugs
that conspire to embezzle millions. In another instance,
a Ukrainian tax inspector who gets paid an equivalent of
10 dollars a month is by nature corruptible, which turns
the entire nation into this endemic recycling corruption
system that exists at different degrees around the globe.
So Viktor Yanukovych wasn't corrupt; he emptied the
Ukrainian coffers, and his action broke the entire
Ukrainian economy. He is merely a scapegoat, for the
twentieth century had innumerable versions of Viktor
Yanukovych; we are going to have more of the same
caliber brutes if we keep patronizing their celebrated
'mentors' in the western hemisphere and ignore the fact
that their schemes led to regional civil and global
financial instabilities that dearly cost us all; as
exemplified by the demise of the Malaysian passengers
aboard the assailed Malaysian airlines Flight MH17.

Mohamed Bouazizi; the name should speak for itself
at this point.

As I cranked the knob of my indignation to higher
decibels from one chapter to another, I massaged your
ears with a few interludes to soften the onslaught of my
rants.

The final episode in this series, "Say WHAAAT?"
was more than a play on French economist Jean-
Baptiste Say's name. I had taken the reader back to the
long forgotten initial crime scene of Capitalism and
excavated a monster. Long after his death, Nassau
Senior's skeleton radiates a green effervescent color as

he planted the festering seed in the latest dominant
form of economy and fiercely played a central role for
profiteers' supremacy over the laboring class. I made it
my mission to desecrate Nassau Senior's grave. Left to
me, for as long as his travesty enslaves us all in this
askew form of enrichment and extravagance,
deactivating rationality, on his tombstone should be
engraved D.R.I.P; don't rest in peace.

"A cat likes to eat fresh fish but it will not go into the
water."

Mongolian Proverb

Even among those who reject economic hysteria, some
warn that a disproportionate distribution of wealth is
harming the middle class. Has my *tour of hell* in the
past hundred pages got you worried? Economists have
poetic theories that blamed high unemployment on a
weak demand for goods and services while the
disgraceful photo of socio-economic disparity is collecting
dust. Here is the real problem: pecuniary gains from
formidable performance increased and the narrowed
distance and time between sellers and buyers on this
planet have been syphoned to the reclusive class, the
profiteers *aka* the capitalists. Amazing technological
jumps from the typewriter to a laptop didn't benefit at
all the real movers and shakers of the factories, I mean
the laboring class, that saw the reclassification of the
term subsistence to what is now called these days a
wage.

I wouldn't protest my beheading if this book was only filled with apocalyptic rage and without an authentically formidable response. If nothing else, I have learned from my shepherd apprenticeship; bold concepts are nerve-wracking for the ignoramus but self-anointed *crème de la crème* as much as it is for the rest of us self-aware idiots. As a result, the approach taken in subsequent chapters is not hauled from the tussle of piecing together a well-thought-of tune. I have tried my best to be as parsimonious as possible to avoid leaving you nauseated and faint from all the new concepts I will throw at you. It was necessary that I took it upon myself to redefine and recalibrate terminologies that are the vital building blocks of my alternative concepts.

From here on out, please take the necessary precautions, especially before delving into *abracadabra*. The end is far from any anticipation, more brutal than you can ever imagine!!!

As you have insistently knocked at the devil gates, you shall come in...

X

Diamonds are a woman's BFF

"Le cœur a ses raisons, que la raison ne connaît point."
Blaise Pascal

A wise man who came face to face with a cobra swore to me that he was more terrified of waking up in the early morning to the fuming gaze of a woman than any venomous reptile. I came to that same conclusion as I slowly opened my eyes one morning to the beautiful melody of the birds near my window, and Tara had her arms and legs crossed. Oh, Shit. Her menacing raccoon eyes were a clear sign that she didn't get any sleep, calibrating this ambush. On a tactical point, I needed to quickly scan through a million scenarios in my mind. So I started to sort through my stockpiled inventory of blunders. The previous night, I was on lockdown in our apartment while she went out partying with her BFFs. There is no way I could be guilty of dragging my sloppy drunk ass to bed and licking her face off all night. Then I verified the sealed trunk of my prior bachelor debauchery years and of sordid memories. Could she have found out that long before we met, I once received fellatio from a deceptive cross-dresser? Hey, in my defense, I wasn't the only one who buried my genitalia in the suspected to be gentleman's mouth.

I was about to spill the beans out loud while begging for forgiveness for my past transgressions when Tara rolled out the laundry list of charges concocted by her brigade of disgruntled female friends. What was I thinking? Nothing good could come out of my girlfriend hanging out with my former bedmate and another non-distant encounter. I pictured the scorned collaborators and the other lonely females spitting out my rap sheet, using my tainted past to place layers of doubt over our flourishing love pact. While these vultures spent the night taking shots of vodka, stepping to Beyonce's songs, did they actually convince Tara that I was no good? To escape the guillotine, I was given one choice; a test of fire. If I really want it, I have to put a ring on it!

If I could only have used the time and money we spent on this selfish pursuit to build a time machine, I would have programmed it to the year 1908, and the destination: Kolmanskop, Namibia. Once there, all I would have to do was bend over, pick one of the shiny stones laying on the floor, and zoom back to the present with a bigger stone than the microscopic diamond we ended up burning my student loan money on. For a moment, I wondered if I would have been as naïve as Zacharies Lewala; he was the man who soon after he picked up a similar sparkling rock that I had envisioned to present to my future wife, he showed it to his German supervisor August Stauch. Lewala was never to be seen again. Maybe I would have been captured? Being black and not suited for endless hours of manual labor, it is probable that I would have been another victim added to the numerous untold accounts of diabolical experiments and tests conducted at the on-site hospital, practicing what Germans would later come to perfect in the concentration camps of Europe.

It pains me now to think about the amount of gas we burned in our car, chasing down the perfect diamond. Adding on to the guilt of our contribution to the extinction of polar bears due to the $CO2$ emissions from our vehicle, is the agonizing torture that I had to endure having to be explained to me, the complexity of the "4 Cs" used to classify diamonds (Carat, Color, Cut, and Clarity). Is this the ultimate expression of love for her? I was disheartened that the numerous romantic poems I wrote, the emptying of my savings, and the hours I put in the kitchen bamming harder than the Bayou chef, Emeril, were dwarfed by this glittering piece of carbon.

As we drove across three counties on the hunt, I pondered how strong the alluring pull that a diamond has; was it more powerful than funny, sweet, romantic, daring, amusing, playful, lovely, and silly memories built with couples around the globe? Was it truly matters of the heart? The logic splendidly elaborated by Adam Smith, David Ricardo, and Karl Marx appears to explain the value bestowed on this metastable allotrope of tiny pieces of carbon. These classical political economists' embellished calibration was rightly hypothesized to conform to the dynamism of the market and velocity of money during their era. Transactions have since evolved at a rapid pace. Money's velocity collides like billiard balls on a pool table, bouncing off in all directions. Neither individuals nor nations trade anymore; now, we sell and buy. Large sums are carried electronically on a plastic card and transcontinental deals are made on a screen with a push of a button or a tap on a smart screen. Twenty-first century technical miracles and multinationals blitzes make the old guard look like the Three Stooges who took it upon themselves to polish up their contemporary spoofs. The irony remains that the exorbitant prices placed on this precious stone has nothing to do with its rarity; diamonds are not as rare as we have been told. The continued mining of diamonds from the earth provides the evidence that renders the old claim as obsolete.

As I was taking down the picture of the Three Stooges of economics down from my office wall, I thought of other ways to rationalize the sustained tyranny of the diamond industry. It is child's play to simply believe that by carefully restricting the supply, De Beers has kept the price of diamonds high. Around 1938, they had a hard time selling stones. Folks either didn't see the use of diamonds or they couldn't afford it. An ingenious consultant, Gerold Lauck, figured out how to hypnotize the western world. The remedy he prescribed was De Beers had to market diamonds as a status symbol and soon after diamonds became the engagement stone of choice. I can rightly attest to the success of Lauck's campaign; I am one of his victims. It would be a clear act of dishonesty to claim that the overbearing pursuit for status is an exclusive sin the planet Earth masters; yet, the west's fascination for the glittery stone has engulfed the rest of us on one end or another.

"Do not bite at the bait of pleasure till you know there is
no hook beneath it."

Thomas Jefferson

I drove around town feeling like the worst person on
earth for the caricaturist depiction of women when it
comes to diamonds and poking fun on the "buddhafied"
economists in the previous passage. My usual method to
chase away my worries and anxiety is getting lost in
Toys"R"Us, the American toy superstore chain which is a
paradise for children and kids at heart like myself. I
spent the entire evening touching toys, video games,
dolls, action figures, learning toys, and building toys.
However, my moment of Zen was abruptly disrupted by
the loud scream of a toddler, hauled out of the store by
an embarrassed mother while this mini Luciano
Pavarotti was ferociously hanging on a Barbie crown.
Right then it dawned on me; if I were to hold back my
deeper thoughts, I would be giving the reader a false
sense that only our edgy desire to set ourselves apart
from the herd, tricks us to pick up rubbish from
department store racks. And if you are reading this line
it means that I am obligated to tell the full story as I
have taken a closer look at the north stars guiding
consumer habits.

Before Harry Gordon Selfridge opened his store in
1908 on Oxford Street in London, stores had floor
managers who stalked their clients and 'politely' tossed
out anyone who was perceived as not being a potential
buyer. People want to forget or never heard that around

the time England was regarded as the most advanced nation on the planet, a proper woman couldn't go out without being chaperoned by a male figure and different social classes could not shop at the same store. Then arrived Selfridge, whose marketing tactics deployed in London England, drawn from years spent climbing the ladder and landing on the top managerial spot of Marshall Field's store over the pond in Chicago, transformed the entire shopping experience and dismantled the cruel practice of literally having indentured employees work and live in the stores full-time. For the first time in England, people of any social background were endorsed to see and touch goods at their own leisure, and women's toilets were built in the store to avoid disrupting the ladies' shopping spree. Selfridges' store not only 'civilized' English society, it also provided a template for the entire retail industry. The clever man probably took to heart his childhood, as a dirt poor kid in rural Wisconsin. His lessons learned from his biblical sessions of the irresistible temptation that led to Adam and Eve's fall from grace, opened the gates for unlimited browsing that exposed humankind's imperfections and pocketbooks.

The unrelenting portrait of Chinese prosperity drawn as a Godzilla attack is erroneous. For starters, Godzilla is a Japanese lizard and nothing like a Chinese dragon; in addition, it is racist to think that all Asian monsters look alike. Not long ago, a xenophobic propaganda rolled up into a film, and caught me off guard. The documentary, *Red Obsession* focuses its attention on how the Wealthy Chinese' lust for the grand cru has altered prices throughout the world supply of high priced wines. While simultaneously, the myopic film obscured the fact that vineyards set prices based on opinion from the industry's supercilious critics, as one of them in the film who asserts that he doesn't just taste wine, he "listens" to it. And the hour long hoop-la wrongly amplified the role played by plump marionettes like Robert Parker, on the French wines invasion of the Chinese market. Anyone can quote me on this, if they dare. Baron Eric de Rothschild's nonstop piss over the Great Wall, reaching footsteps of the Chinese who amassed a fortune throwing dildos over the wall to the west, cracked the curious nature of the Chinese appetite.

Scarcity is a term that western civilizations have abused extensively by all industry sectors and its impact in the economic field has had far-reaching repercussions. Yet, it is not enough to turn a product into a cash cow. Large retail chains with their global tentacles have unlocked and mastered the second value that I am sculpting this time around. I believe that leaving a Walmart superstore without purchasing anything is not only reckless but immoral; well, unless it is after midnight and you are a beautiful single female wearing a skimpy outfit. In the war waged against deep pockets and parasite conglomerations, for the mom and pop stores, it's now a matter of survival. Buying into the same cunning pattern of flooding us with products and advertisements in a deceptive confusing way with a charming American southern accent or the unreliable head rotations of Ganesh.

In a guise to make a product a commercial victory for the sake of a businesses' longevity, labelled as competiveness, from the old era when humans started taking advantage of another's limitations to the new era of corporations taking advantage of our flaws, commerce boils down to one element; bringing a product within potential customers' physical reach, and these days, within our digital range is a vital.

> "Should I kill myself, or have a cup of coffee?"
>
> Albert Camus

"Two down, one more to go!" I said to myself. As I was letting my family jewels hang out to catch a breeze on my bureau and patted myself on the back for banging out two cornerstones of my consumer behavior analysis, a dilemma of painting a clear picture to the last push that will give birth to subsequent chapters, suddenly arose and deflected my ego. Throughout the book, I came to routinely set the décor of my ratiocinations, expending on my own life and abusing family members and friends to gauge a reader's interest. To my credit, it is not every day that you run into somebody who has in their childhood, assisted in any authoritarian regime's best solution to anything written off as social ill, public execution. Yes, I have watched brutal criminals, strong-willed activists, and political prisoners suffocating and jerking as they dangled on a foregone hope for hours until their necks gave up. Then again, these spectacles weren't applauded or widely embraced as the slick guillotine during the French revolution's Reign of Terror. These crimes weren't the reflection of a community as authorities sponsored lynching shows in the southern regions of United States during the Jim

Crow era where law-enforcement would hold a suspected Negro captive until a white mob formed and enforced social conventions. I have yet to understand how insanity and a sense of duty wins over reason; but I am overwhelmed by the defiance of the condemned.

I have dreamed about the moment I would take on the vital viewpoint that goes beyond consumerism. Sadly, I realized that I was oblivious of the steep mountain I had to climb in the effort of awakening readers' sense of right and wrong throughout the last leg of my exposé. Boiling deep inside me was an impassive resistance as it became apparent that I would have to dig out the most miserable experiences of my childhood to shed a light on living beings envied trait. I surely doubt that the reason of my vain break out from hell would add clarity to this *tête-à-tête* dialogue you and I are having right now. Trying to clear the way through tons of hatred memorabilia in my mind and then to extract the pure partum of my troubles and tribulations, I shall say that having spent nights on top of a Coca-Cola stand and failing to experience Buddha's final extinguishment opened my eyes to our inability to just lay down and die, without the help of a sympathetic Doctor Kevorkian.

Tales of misery are already in abundance in this book, but there is also more than the sliver of tales of survival and plenty to say about the driving force behind our mental restraint that prevents us from choking a micromanaging supervisor or a loudmouthed customer at work. More than any species, humans have mastered the action steps required to avoid pain or to prolong our existence. There is no doubt in my mind we all have the same resolve of satisfying our individual needs but the difference is the fact that we go about it different ways. My older cousin Claude, a kleptomaniac, has never held a job for more than two days in his entire existence, but somehow he manages to live very well, rubbing elbows with the rich and the famous, by means of his talent. There is another trigger to why we buy what we buy. In addition, or apart to sentiment and temptation, in the purchase of a shoe, getting a shelter, going to work, eating food, or simply put , hanging on or smoothing life, I see a response to *our inability to sustain discomfort and fear to face the unknown after death.*

"I have striven not to laugh at human actions, not to weep at them, nor to hate them, but to understand them"

Baruch Spinoza

My conspiracy theorist friends have liken this chapter to a ride on a an accelerated steel roller coaster, when used in an attempt to explain abuses, financial crisis, wars, and the world population's growing waistlines. What else to expect when the complicity of humans' propensity of actions lays interchangeably with Machiavellian tactics and insatiable curiosity. I assert creatures' pursuit of satisfaction is based on a contingency scale, while the notion of material needs and maximizing pleasure are flamboyant fables lobbed by theorists in a desire to secure their academic positions. I have painstakingly organized this chapter in a way to be effortlessly consumed, and I am well aware that the three concepts I have elucidated will be washed away from the reader's mind if not given clichéd labels and summarized.

Sentimental value: Grandparents, coked-up parents, and overbearing mothers capitalize on the hypnotizing power of sentimental coercion and a person subjected to this radioactive ray for a long time suffers from acute low self-esteem, need of reaffirmation, and diabetes. These purely psychological *necessities* that can be manufactured by our own phantasms or marketing scams.

Proximity value: A number of the creation tales that suggest women are to blame for all the human suffering in the world today; not at all, I say! We have all inherited Pandora's weaknesses; in Greek mythology, god handed her a box and said she was not to open it, she opened it and released all diseases and evils into the world. Temptation is one side of the coin, on the other, there is proximity.

Sustenance value: Throughout time, sustenance value was confined and reduced in the subsistence echelon where we observed in England of Nassau Senior's laborers were given just enough food for another day of work or tossed to the parish. The blame and responsibility is commonly put on capitalists; unrelated to Thorstein Veblen's assaults on the nouveau rich and conspicuous consumption, I turned the finger around and keeping the blood flow through our veins, there is an independent motive behind the universal subordination to the narrow definition of physiological *necessaries*.

I have to underline <u>propensity of action</u> as a key to my analysis. To tie everything together and throw a bone to people who have failed to solve this riddle of the universe, lacking ketamine to make the journey into the obscure mind, *propensity of action* the opposite of <u>indifference</u> is the sum of values (sentimental, proximity, and sustenance). To reassure the reader, I have shortened this perplexing explanation for a visual reason, and in subsequent chapters, I will put this concept on a commerce pedestal and illuminate structural implications.

However, there are certain vital points to express about values' characteristics.

Fluidity: No other journey illustrates it better than how a psychological play can turn into a physiological entrapment than drug addiction. From an aggressive teenager's social pot smoking to fit in a group of the tragic adult life of a full blown crack head. Walking barefoot can seem to be the sexiest 'bohemian' thing to do on a U.S. campus, we have shoes to avoid the painful blisters that harden our soles, but Kanye West implies that a pair of overpriced Gucci tennis shoes makes you fly.

Zero or negative: As we were growing up, one my dearest friends was considered as the weirdest kid in our group. He had zero interest in girls, other than braiding their hair. After more than a decade later, I ran into him while vacationing and cruising through my old neighborhood. He is unabashedly, flamingly gay. And his hair was impeccably coiffed.

Going back to the initial story, the treasure hunt didn't end the way my wife expected. As she was parading her ring around the city to her friends, she racked up more awful reactions and cynical comments than applause. One of her friends whispered a shocking thought, questioning if the ring was a blood diamond. To my great satisfaction, she has since torched her VIP membership of the mean girls' club card, and on Facebook, she downgraded all of her BFF's relationship status to acquaintances. Let's be real for a moment here; not only I am a prime catch for a sexy nurse who takes the pain of working on tormented and ill souls, but the status symbol of wearing a ring indicates being revered as someone precious and worthy of claiming is far more appealing than the routine sexual sprinting nightmare single females endure in the rummage waiting for their other halves. Simply put, sentiments are manufactured. And as long as a potential storylines could be engraved on these piece of carbon, crooks dangle it right in front of our eyes, and engagement sanctifies fleshly pleasures, diamonds will be men's ghastly fantasy and women's true BFFs!

XI

Hop-o'-My-Thumb

"I stopped looking for a Dream Girl, I just wanted one
that wasn't a nightmare."
Charles Bukowski

After exchanging jabs and hooks in this book, I'm sure that you feel like you are on the receiving end of an abusive relationship. If those tale-tell signs haven't scared you away, hell, I bet confessions of my wild days wouldn't. Friends and family members' adjustment to my alcohol and party phobia has been dawdling. It seems not long ago no matter where I was on this planet, no matter what single or pseudo committed horny dogs I was with, or hanging out with my cousin Oliver, the weekend was dedicated to lewd and opaque celebrations.

Where is the singles spot where impulsive predators and diverse preys converge? Nightclubs! But even packed like sardines, different squads draw demarcating lines that make the hunt for a bedmate extremely exasperating. From Manshiet Nasser garbage city in Egypt to the flashy appearance of Dubai's financial center, booze induced brave men peruse the landscape;

enduring the same pains of making the first move by offering a drink to their object of interest, ultimately puts them in a weaker bargaining position. Whereas voracious for copious amounts of free spirits, the crafty women stay seductively vague and just out of reach while afflicting severe damage to the novice players' bar tabs.

I am not a stranger to humiliating and crushing defeats in the nightclub scene. With failure comes experience, or I should say, I've developed new strategies. There is an age and time a predator goes through the process of learning how to synchronize 'both heads' in the game. Slaps on my face and petty deceits sharpened my German Shepherd nose and sniper instincts. Now, I can easily sniff out a not so undercover slut right off the waiting line outside a nightclub who is easily persuaded that jumping in a total stranger's car is a wise decision. For the sake of my life, my wife, and a mob of pretend to be nice dudes who might kill me, as well as for the continuity of the male species, I have to assert that not every man yearns for a bimbo. It was my wonderful and stress-free *preference*, at the time!

When it comes to mating, the female species have their own quirks. My female pals, a melting hot pot of diverse backgrounds and races, are either pathologic liars, or they suffer from a disjunction of the brain and the rest of the body. They claim to seek for tall, attractive, wealthy, and well educated partners. This prototype chosen one, the alpha male, is a mocking contrast to the midget clowns, broke wild boars, or females they usually vanish with playing drunk after leaving the club. When I ask my now wife, why she

consented to dating me and marrying me, the
ingredients of the foolish elixir became to me,
surprisingly simple. The prime downfall of these
tigresses is summed up to relentless nuisance, aloof
boldness, and shady humor. The three hypnotizing
forces break females' indifference, and voila!

On the surface, every agent in the club doesn't want
to go home alone. Ironically, ladies don't parade half
naked around to meet men and are indifferent to the
plethora of guys asking for their numbers whereas
gentlemen flock to clubs to meet women of their
preferences and there is never a shortage of prospects.
The same equation is applied to the cyber world and
extended to casual strolls down a busy street where
males initiate a chat based on what they see and a
female response is based on how they feel at the
moment. In a party, this picture comes to life when
someone divulges in a conversation on their own
dating saga, and boom, females unilaterally claim
chivalry is dead and put the blame on males while
males unanimously counteract by dumping the blame
on females because their prospects are to play hard to
get.

Right now, you have probably chuckled long
enough, and are wondering how this shameless wooing
contest ties into economics. I'll push aside the
complexities of same-sex relationships and other forms
of relationships in an effort to be succinct. Men's
propensity to act is based to great extent on their
sustenance values, a preference, and women's
propensity to act is driven by their sentimental values,

an indifference. Proximity values are weighted the same on the propensity to act for both genders. In terms of commerce, I cannot support the false microeconomic premise of *preference* and *indifference* that lecturers use to daze their students and have made it their bread and butter. The dissection of club scenes is the same as the market. Allow me to attribute a gender without assigning the prejudice that comes with it; a firm is male and the customer is a female.

My assertions invoke a simplicity in the complex samba dance between firms and consumers. On one hand, company chair boards, which are still exceptionally dominated by egotistic males, make a decision based solely on the survival and continuity objective which is subjected to preferences. An enterprise or business consists of a group of people or an individual in search for cash cow products or 'gains' and act as men in the club. Mass manipulation is not exempted by this rule; Bangladesh's Prime Minister Sheikh Hasina or the former United States Secretary of State Hillary Rodham Clinton, impersonate male machoism to play in the big leagues. On the other hand, women have inherited the critical responsibility of our wellbeing. From early age, children of both genders are dragged though bazaars and freezing superstores, and are constantly exposed to our mothers' buying patterns. Therefore, it is not a surprise that this brain programming process has come to define buyers' capricious decision making in the market, or simply put it, our indifferences.

In the western hemisphere, you would be amazed
the length firms go to seduce consumers and break
their indifference. Entire store floors are designed
based on sophisticated studies of consumers'
behaviors. The same principal goes for the less refined
and in your face method of street merchants in the
voodoo markets in Lome, Togo or the floating Asian
markets of Bangkok Thailand. While businesses are
working hard to let down our guards and open up our
pockets, we, the consumers of any gender, age, race,
geographic location and social stratification, including
Vladimir Vladimirovich Putin, turn into little girls.

"The hardest thing to explain is the glaringly evident
which everybody had decided not to see."

Ayn Rand

In the western hemisphere, I am dazed by the
unparalleled general public's naivety. The idleness to
promptly fact check information might have something
to do with the amount of easily accessible news. Facing
any problem, it is important for me to drill down to the
source and catch the snake by its tail. Akin to 1878,
Milton Wright brought to his two youngest sons,
Wilbur and Orville, a toy "helicopter" made of paper.
The Wright brothers went on to build a flying
machine. This story sounds so romantic but it is not
without controversy and competing claims; I have in
mind Gustave Whitehead. I pin on these mechanical
bird fathers, the Nippon's atrocious attack on Pearl
Harbor and the American government's extreme

retaliation with the atomic bomb on Hiroshima and
Nagasaki. I imagine every party involved have
assumed new identities in hell to avoid a second death
by a mob lynching for their contribution to the death of
our beautiful planet.

Every now and then, I subject my intellect to
bizarre cage fights, seeking to improve my tolerance of
ill-informed individuals. No matter how stylishly I
defeated a Shaolin impersonator, it is never great for
people who come from countries that I view as locked
in the search of understanding others instead of
seeking to uncover who they truly are. Needless to say,
I have no sympathy for these agnostics and slaves
whose pigheadedness are prolonging their nations'
economic quashicore. Their complacency lays in the
internationally chanted and exaggerated excuse of
civil conflicts and corruption, and for the case of
Native American tribes, alcoholism.

Coming from one of the publicized degenerated
republics, a country like many others where the switch
was used on instead of being placated with benefits
during The United States fear of Communism during
the sixties and seventies, I have the right to say it has
been long overdue that we face the glaring truth.
Discounting the effects on formerly colonized nations
of the "assumed" role of the government and its
leadership as a sage parent providing for his
dependent brood, inherited from the lingering
molesting habits of colonization, herds of pitiable
scholars suggests that the third world nations' most
pressing issue is unemployment; and for that I say its
two cures are a thousand miles further down the road

of Adam Smith's division of labor. The prevailing heterogeneous national advanced skill trade specialization or the way I like to call it: "Fake it until you make it, yours". The other solution is consequential to the twenty-first century: The learning systems' pluralism.

I have painstakingly expounded on class recompense and the learning system's pluralism in the last chapter of this book, so hold on for that part. Let's take baby steps. The heterogeneous national trade specialization infancy stage requires building infrastructure and carving a *main d'oeuvre*; essentially, money to concoct the medicine and to conduct painful sessions of economic chemotherapy. If your nation has nukes, please balloon your debt to finance steroid injections and get huge fast. In mid-2014 the world debt has reached to $59 trillion dollars! And shockingly (I'm being facetious), the highest debtors are not the impoverished Chad and war infested Republic of Central Africa, but the lionized United States and United Kingdom economies.

Why isn't anyone advising the former United Kingdom's Prime Minister Tony Blair under his current alias, Transparency International, to quit barking on the poor and bite on his own tail? Nonetheless world, don't panic. With the offset of other countries, there is another $370 billion dollars to waste before we all jump off this planet! Let me turn my attention to the countries without any nukes or any terrifying military arsenals, my personal advice is to avoid the self-enslavement trap and financial institutions tyranny by opting out from the foreign investments shackles and take the contractors route. Those who are willing to be a private tutor like Fred C. Koch, just make sure they don't have evil kids.

Other countries simply pump on steroids which have dangerous health consequences, such as political balls shrinkage or the exacerbation of the leadership's delusions. The latter happened to Mexico; the forced modernization and economic growth under José de la Cruz Porfirio Díaz Mori's reign should serve here as a cautionary tale. Porfirio created a gaping disparity between the blossoming higher class and severe impoverishment of the rural masses that led to the Mexican revolution of 1910.

After all the hard work, a country will fall ill with the powerful economic degenerative disk joint disease. There are plenty of accounts showing as a nation becomes wealthy, the success reveals ongoing socio-economic challenges, the central tune in this book. What is it? If you have figured it out, great. For the slackers, I categorically refuse to do all the mental work for you. Let's just hope that you will be able decipher it by the end of this chapter or you are doomed.

After months of introspection, it still makes no sense the lasting imposition of David Ricardo's flawed dismemberments of commerce and especially trade over political economy. The fact that Ricardo's comparative advantage is taught with rigor, places economic academia's passivity onto full display. But my concern is of another spectrum. I am not surprised by the skill as a broker and prosperous financial

market speculator that Ricardo was, to stumble on one
right bet that has undone most of his wrongs.
Ricardo's deduction of the duality between labor cost
and profit was indeed a small statement for man, one
giant observation for mankind!

I view the direct inverse relationship between labor
and profit a natural law as gravity forces. Yet I
articulate it differently, ducking the cardinal sin made
by classical economists of fusing together two distinct
activities. I have to soften on this accusation because
of the premise in their simplified examples, beaver and
deer in the case of Adam Smith; commodities are
exchanged and not sold in an open market place. In
addition, money wasn't yet the crucial utensil
representing a share of a nation's wealth and
sophistically tied to welfare. To make this clear, I don't
suggest that money represents the invisible amount of
energy dispensed to catch and bring deer on the
market, but money is a transferrable instrument
piecing contributions to the general welfare. My
example is a nation for which the entire economy is
based on making chairs. If this nation has one
hundred chairs, the volume of any transportable form
of payment backed by this nation's government
represents roughly the one hundred chairs.

If you can't read between the lines, I meant
monetary policy can only staunch an economic
hemorrhage, but will never revive or increase a
nation's economic virility. Nonetheless, I am not going
to ignore money as a financial instrument that
artificially creates more money. And the dollar isn't an

exemption. Yet, America efficaciously knocked out gold and by substituting gold with the golden sealed dollar as the world's currency reserve, slowly swamped and controlled other nations' wealth representation or in our example the number of chairs. The subtle message in this chapter, is to refute the notion of rational maximizer and rather demonstrate that humans just as any other creature is a rational minimizer. We use information that is available to us and a priori experience to pursue the goal of minimizing our risk, our disappointment, and our pain in every choice that we make. However, the value that has greater influence on our decision making process is fundamentally based on the role we assume at the time; either as prey or predator. When you go to a supermarket, you are the prey and when you are selling something, your are the predator. While I am on this exercise of defining terms that you will be encountering in subsequent passages, I shall warn you that price is used here as *a pecuniary gain relative to a person's propensity to act, regardless if it is a commodity of just price, market price, or natural price.*

My graceful round of applause to Ricardo has led my mind into a thought-provoking labyrinth. Please hold tight, I am going to try my best not to lose you. The best way of telling this story without losing you goes, as Capitalism in its current form, holds a conflictual bridge between production and service. Revenue is determined by the supply side. Capitalists first atrophy of labor's sustenance value, rendered labor cost into a fixed labor price to collect a hefty

share of the just price; and then they crossed over to
the demand side, abusing the terrified labor to squeeze
out the maximum of the profit while tricking
consumers' sentimental value to raise the market price
as high as the natural price and as they can get away
with.

From my observation of one person living in an
atrocious slum and another in a gated community,
both go to work to maintain a roof over their heads
and each one of them owns a television set and a DVD
player because they love watching salacious movies.
This example is not to assume that poor people like to
emulate opulence, but dully pointing out principles
enslaving humans to work like mules and to
consumerism are equitably and universally scattered.
In fact, Karl Marx's exploitation of labor denunciation
was modestly right and, at the same time, somehow
wrong for not placing alongside the exploitation of
consumers.

Brave foxes like the Ricardian Socialist Thomas
Hodgskin fell flat on their pasty faces, by stretching
Ricardo's centerpiece and declared that labor is the
source of all value. This is a classic *réponse du berger
à la bergère* to bourgeois proponents edict and the
current stand that capitalists endure the entire risk in
commerce. For any fervent Karl Marx supporters
reading this book; I am sincerely sorry, but I have
ceased to regard this drunk, short tempered, bearded
man as a maverick for his disorienting concession that
laborers are lost without moneyers. Coupled with
Piero Sraffa's longwinded and meager contribution to

dust out Ricardo's idea, has only added to the
complexity of the argument enough to secure a number
of economic faculty's existence. For the most part,
David Ricardo's only correct argument, the duality
between labor and profit, has been lost under a bunch
of rubbish theories.

"Do not scare the birds you are going to shoot."

Malagasy Proverb

There is a subscribed effort in our general conscience to
mute the debate around economic disparities. The few
times that the microphone volume was switched on,
discussions have been centered on who is well deserving
or undeserving to get the lion's share of the surplus. In
fact, the finger wrestling games have lost their
popularity before cruising through the twenty-first
century. I can imagine soon, people will be turning to
sorcerers to advise economic policies, like African and
Haitian leaders have been doing for years. Who is to
blame for the lack of originality when it comes to solving
this dilemma from the economics discipline?

Economists have been tiptoeing around the defining
line between the initial two Capitalism sectors,
production and service, in their allocutions on their
inaccurate definition of natural price and market price
while fearing only the latter contains a justifiable
surplus. Yet in the lone star state of Texas, the spoiled
brat electrical car manufacturer, Tesla, is not allowed to
sell its vehicles directly to the public. Automakers have
to go through franchised dealers to offer their products
and services. While in Ethiopia, I find out restaurants

cannot own a butcher shop or vice versa. Around the world, there are blatant illuminated walls erected between production and service based on common sense without thwarting business sectors.

I was once told by *lumpenintellectuals* hanging onto their outdated and deflated fame, that I had no right to pick up where David Ricardo has left off until they approved that I was well deserving to embark on such a journey. So far, I keep finding breadcrumbs with David Ricardo's initials on every one I have picked up. Fuck your consent; I have nothing to lose following the crumb trail and preaching the message of deliverance before monetary gangsters manufacture another deceitful 'economic recovery boom' and persuade the world that change is not needed.

As today's world is full of applications on our smartphones that make the invention of the remote prehistoric and threatens to gnaw away at my father-in-law's tax filing business, there is no excuse for blindly charging down the wrong path. Joseph Schumpeter is one of the exotic rare birds who voiced their concern on the role of ideology in economics, but more importantly, he foresaw a glimpse of the miracle; as it is presented today, information systems' advancement has since demystified the role of bank tellers, darkened the future of accountants, and extended financial transactions into real-time constancy to far-reaching corners of Earth. I have a great conviction that the objective of the advancement of technology is to bridge the gap between the deplorable *what is* and the incredible *what ought to be.*

Interlude V

I am not so talented to put into words

I am trying to erase the space between us

The perfect story will have to wait

while we load the wooden line

with all realities flaring out

I write one based on that I would have to say

it is just too complex for my mind to scheme

see, my hands are trying to hold

what I could not imagine before

and what I can't seem to word, people

is the full effect of me in your head

and I do not even know why I would want to

except that I hear you

and maybe not even that

this is bigger than the words I can pronounce

It is my every day, for as long as I lost my imagination

and I do not apologize

for not knowing how to describe it

as it is in full

as it is in flesh

as it is...

a miracle, certainly

a sacrifice, indeed

One thing is for sure

I treasure my pen and my pain

for the sake of this

I will not give up the thoughts to honor this

no,

I will not give up trying

to chase the devil away

XII

Current and rude state of society

"Dì il vero e affronterai il diavol"

Italian Wisdom

Never before have I been moved like the first time I read the last paragraph of the eleventh chapter of what I consider to be the economist's Torah, The Wealth of Nations. Right there, Adam Smith delivered a poignant sermon denouncing the avid character of profiteers. He prophesied an economic deluge to come if the profiteer class wasn't kept well in check and would eventually produce the Ivar Kreugers, Sibtul Shahs, and the Bernard Madoffs that we see today. I imagine that Smith's spirit is flying around, frantically ringing the alarm. If there is something to learn from the recurring waves of the global financial crisis, it is that the public's consciousness is at all times, trailing a thousand steps behind business owners' conniving chess moves to fuse wealth and power. The Nostradamus of political economy lived long enough to get a glimpse of the building momentum preceding his spine-chilling nightmare of the untamable global financial upheaval.

Two centuries ago, Smith's apprehensions of
"moneyers" cozying up to the creatures addicted to
power and parades (politicians), have long been derided
by the presumptuous sense that self-interests and social
responsibility are not mutually exclusive ideals. In
reality, the phony democratic antagonistic ritual of
elections, lures candidates of all denominations and
platforms in need of campaign funds and ammos into the
wicked tycoons' sound proof dungeons. The victors will
remain in that dungeon on a short leash during their
term in office, where they are slapped around with
pillows filled with cash while standing still and
powerless, viewing through their peep-hole their
'sponsors' beating the crap out of Main Street to beat
Wall Street's expectations. Yet these abuses of public
trust don't come close to the brutality and repression
experienced in the somber hemisphere. In countries
where the dividing line between the two worlds, public
and private, is non-existent and politics is synonymous
with business, really bad things happen all the time to
really good people and life goes on.

On tax, Smith's psychic clairvoyance was also right
on point. Conglomerations, with their tentacles around
the globe have mastered in truncating their tax
obligation so well with cooked up exemptions to the
point where public treasuries end up owing them money.
The number of tiny islands pimped out as tax havens
has exploded, making it easy for people and businesses
who can hire a nerdy accountant and change their
continent of residence to evade taxes. We have nothing
to be proud of. Recent pushback from the United
Kingdom's government against the hulk known as

Starbucks, ingeniously exercised businesses' protection to evade tax and the assault launched by the most indebted nation on this galaxy onto secretive Swiss banks. Both nations have no intention to level the playing field for all. Proof? In the United States, all I need is to hit the road and get to Delaware to hide my twelve dollars from Uncle Sam; if you were aware of it, Joe Biden's state is a secrecy jurisdiction.

Now I must regain my composure; the triumphal drum beats of the New Orleans funeral parade honoring Adam Smith's gutsy allocution to ensure future generations don't endure misery and pain stop right here!

> "You know you're an alcoholic when you misplace things ... like a decade."
>
> Paul Williams

I hope that by now, you have deciphered the subliminal parental advisory warning label I plugged into the book's introduction, and please be aware that the explicit content of this passage is intended to pull the mask off Adam Smith, and to reveal the horrible side of this celebrated Scottish moral philosopher and a pioneer of political economy. The subsequent adverse effects that you will likely experience includes serious verbal diarrhea, and if your vision gets blurry, don't call an economist. Much ink has been spilled on Smith's non-conventional lifestyle and afflictions, but I found Smith competent to stand trial for his cerebral supernatural ability to perceive events in the future throughout The

Wealth of Nations' thousand pages. In one disgraceful move, Adam Smith cast a shameful shadow on his scholarly dedication to integrity and social progress. And the weight of his mistake is heavily felt in every occupation's delusional parkour.

Speaking of occupation...

I can remember as if it was yesterday, when my life was turned upside down. For the first time in my entire existence, I had to get a job. If you have ever had to wash a hearse for money, then we have shared the same humiliating chill I feel going down my spine as I write this. I vacuumed and washed cars under the unforgiving Floridian sun all day for tips, and for a quarter of the legal hourly minimum wage. A friend took pity on my disintegrating soul, and hooked me up with a job at a gas station. There I was a rising star, for stocking up the subzero coolers and leaving the store floor spotless after the completion of my night shift. Yet slaving away didn't get me out of this black hole where I constantly had to chase after drunk college kids and to open the safe with a pistol pointed on my forehead. By chance, a customer much admired my awareness of world affairs, and recommended me to Florida's capital city's most coveted office.

I landed a temporary position, three dimes above a minimum wage, but I took immense pride in pulling paper clips on an eight hour shift. Even though the work environment was relatively laid back when a southern boy supervisor wasn't cruising the hall like a shark every day, I looked forward to clocking out and taking advantage of the state employee status perks. I relished the ritual of displaying my badge in plain view, resulting in folks addressing me a proper "Sir" or "Mr." In stores, I received high praises and discounts, and the admiration I received from the African immigrant community catapulted. More importantly, this plastic ID card was a horseshoe magnet for females in search of a man "who's got his act together". I shamelessly wore my badge, even in parties and clubs; no shame in my game!

Even after climbing up the organizational ladder while enduring sporadic moments of racism from every side, blacks included, I never felt well deserving of my pay. Looking back, I really panicked when offered a higher position within the department, which surpassed my fantasized plateau of making twenty dollars per hour. Little that I knew, my terror is a modern triumph sign of the fantastic, well-coordinated coercion mechanism built on classical economists' blasphemy. When it came down to drawing the fundamental principles of Capitalism's new world order and change the course of humanity's social balance, Adam Smith scored against labor and helped to unleash the same profiteers ambitions he decried in the last paragraph of The Wealth of Nations eleventh chapter.

Adam Smith's take on wage is an amenable arrangement in the form of a fair recompense, given by a master to labor laborers. It is important to point out a master implies that somebody who dictates the outcome of the interaction with enslaved laborers by and large, with a visible strong hand. This sentiment resonates with the general repulsive consensus at the time where

European nations were dividing the world and
appropriating distant inhabited territories as they saw
fit, that disastrously resulted in Leopold II's snatching of
an African parcel eighty times bigger than his own tiny
kingdom; and we know the rest of the story. Then again,
how can we continue to justify the current bracket pay
based on the same old notion of subsistence, as a
measure of one's life is worth more than another? No
different from Adam Smith's time, today, blue collar
laborers, corporate go-go dancers, and modern day
slaves' wages are still viewed as compensation or
advances and the master's will is imposed with the same
old firm hand.

There is a universal and classless intuitive sense of
displeasure and discontentment of our present moment
or state, inciting our quest for physical and/or
psychological fulfillment. The proof is in the pudding!
Case in point, the surge in popularity and utilization of
social media and information sharing websites and
applications like Facebook and Instagram, leaving
Amazon and Alibaba in the dust. That insatiable desire
to critique one's current status and compare it to others
is not a new phenomenon. However, existing economic
sermons and models have chosen to ignore that
enterprises have become really good at breaking
children, adults, and old folks' indifference. This
sentiment that emboldened Mansa Abu Bakr to sail west
into the ocean and Charles Darwin to embark on a five-
year voyage on HMS Beagle, made Siddhārtha Gautama
seek enlightenment and Alexander the Great gallop
across continents is so vague and depends enormously
on contingency that economists allowed themselves to

relegate this trap to consumerism instead of understanding it as information seeking behavior.

After long hours of staring at spreadsheets at work, I met up with my burned and disenchanted crew of drinking buddies over to the hottest spot in town, for liquor shots. An eviction notice just reminded one of my friends, who was recently laid off and had fallen behind with his mortgage payments, that he doesn't own his house; the Bank of America does. That was a downer. Let me shed a light onto one groups' misconceived hymn. The emblematic quest for a fancy rooftop and money to splurge on necessities is a universal desire. Yet we have come to believe that entrepreneurship is coded into the DNA of the few, and for the rest us, the only way to legally attain our own utopian dream is self-enslavement. The faster we climb this mountain, the happier tax and debt collectors get, but the further away our ascent to the summit of seventh heaven becomes. As I was drunkenly admiring the number of awards I had received throughout my career as an analyst, I suddenly realized that not only had I become an alcoholic, but a workaholic as well. Alas, all I had to show for after ten years of chasing the carrot like a dummy, was a wall full of colorful plaques!

"The deed is everything, the glory is naught"
Johann Wolfgang Von Goethe

During my childhood in Zaire, while my friends flew overseas for vacations in Europe, my cousins and I were dragged to spend Christmas and New Year's on my grandparents' ranch in Ntamugenga, a small village in what is now eastern DRC (Democratic Republic of Congo). I remember my first night there, where I learned the value of matches. Being one of the most utilized objects in rural DRC, I long envied the inventor of this tool that my dear grandma cherished, for I assumed that the inventor and his offspring became rich off this invention. Little did I know of the ill-fated reality of Janos Irinyi. As a Hungarian chemist in 1836, he mixed phosphorus with lead and gumiarabicum, poured the paste-like mass into a jar, and dipped pine sticks into the mixture and let them dry. He had invented the match. Unfortunately, he lacked the funds for the production of his invention so the poor student turned to Istvan Romer, a rich Hungarian, who bought the invention and its production rights. Istvan Romer became even wealthier off Irinyi's invention whereas the inventor himself died penniless.

The odious crimes of Capitalism that we have become all too familiar with, leave a long list of growing casualties in its wake. They are the faceless men, women, and children, butchered to maintain the price of a commodity, as long as it can remain 'profitable'. We don't pay attention to the many inventors, who have been used as expendable timber to keep the steam train moving. No one is really to blame for Socrates, the Greek philosophical genius, who died totally broke because he refused to accept payment for teaching the young men of Athens. This is different from Philo Taylor Farnsworth, an American inventor who got his modern television invention stolen by Vladimir Zworykin, a scientist for the electronics company RCA. Although Farnsworth won

the court case, in many history books, Zworykin is still
recorded as the inventor of the television. Farnsworth
later received royalties from RCA for his patents, yet the
fact that you never heard about him, demonstrates that
he never gained the recognition that he deserved. This
story is far less tragic than that of Nikola Tesla,
arguably one of the most brilliant scientists of this
millennium. He is the guy that you should love to hate
for your extortionate electrical bill. At the conclusion of
his life in 1943, his body was retrieved from a room in
the New Yorker Hotel, where he had lived his final years
after being evicted from another hotel for not paying his
bill.

The point is not that inventors have the unlucky
penchant for running into really unsavory and greedy
individuals, rather it is capitalist culture, built onto two
pillars that was, is, and will always be: cheap labor and
blue inventors. This patent and start-up fund trap
incites the notorious illicit enrichment of bastards like
Graham Bell, Albert Einstein, Thomas Edison, and
Alexander Fleming who pilfered ideas from Antonio
Meucci, Henri Poincaré, Nikola Tesla, and Ernest
Duchesne, respectively. And let me remind you that
North African tribesmen have been using penicillin to
treat infections for thousands of years.

Foundations, a trend set by Rockefeller and
Vanderbilt, have since become the hippest form of
altruistic behavior of wealthy 'do-gooders'. Who can dare
scoff at someone who racks up immense wealth and then
turns around and gives half of it away? Then again, is
this an illuminating truth that a desire for maximum

wealth accumulation is so futile? Do you think that it is an egotistical character trait to win it all then turn around, open your palace windows and toss it out to watch the commoners scramble to pick it up? Or is it the characteristic of some people who feel the need of grasping the bigger piece of the pie, and play god and dictate what cause needs to be championed and who needs to be saved. I am perplexed, so I call out all those billionaire hipsters to respond to my ruminations for their motives behind this behavior.

I have torpedoed profiteers throughout this book, but I will also admit that the Ponzi scheme is an offshoot of Capitalism that also preys on the rich. Before Bernard Madoff, the financial crooks had a formidable player named Ivar Kreuger a.k.a the "Match King," a Swedish businessman who ran an ingenious pyramid scheme where he monopolized a majority of the world's match industry. When his company went kaput in 1932, wealthy individuals over the globe lost millions in what was The United States largest bankruptcy of its time. This economic blow led to the passage of laws requiring mandatory audits of all companies with listed securities. While we are on the topic of Ponzi schemes, we can make a quick stop to 1979 and check the case of Alberto Vilar who was head of an investment advisory firm that grew to be worth $1 billion. Unfortunately for him, the stock market crash of 2000 virtually erased his fortune. But Vilar was still a generous supporter of the arts, and generously gave hundreds of millions of dollars. Before you feel sorry for the bastard, it was later discovered that Vilar was stealing money from his clients to fund his philanthropic urges.

Ever wondered how many countries were affected by the pilfering of Bernard Madoff? I am going to list these countries starting by the most to least affected, and it is up to you to count them: United States, Germany, Italy, France, Switzerland, Austria, Spain, The Netherlands, United Kingdom, Taiwan, Canada, Mexico, Brazil, Argentina, Chile, Uruguay, Paraguay, Venezuela, Colombia, Peru, Ecuador, Bolivia, Guatemala, Panama, Costa Rica, El Salvador, Honduras, Nicaragua, Belize, Kazakhstan and Georgia, China, Malaysia, Thailand, Singapore, Hong Kong, Taiwan, South Korea, the Philippines, Indonesia, Vietnam, Cambodia, Australia, New Zealand, India, Pakistan, Kuwait, the United Arab Emirates, Qatar, Bahrain, Saudi Arabia, Oman, Lebanon, Turkey, South Africa, Kenya, Egypt, Zimbabwe, Zambia, Mozambique, Angola, Nigeria, Ghana, Senegal, Benin, Cote d'Ivoire, Liberia, Mauritius, Morocco, Algeria, Madagascar, Monaco, Gibraltar, Andorra, Lichtenstein, the Channel Islands, the Isle of Man, Cyprus, Malta, the British Virgin Islands, Bermuda, the Bahamas, Curacao and the Cayman Islands. And for the sake of page space, add to that list, a few tinier Caribbean island nations and virtually every country who is a member of the European Union!

Capitalisms' inherent cannibalism has chewed up some of the wealthiest people. Please research on your own time, Daniel Drew, a 19th century contemporary of Commodore Cornelius Vanderbilt, who died indigent and receiving charity from a church he started. In addition, Horace A.W. Tabor who made millions from his silver mines, but the repeal of the Silver Purchase Act changed his luck for the worse; he was forced to work at a post office to make ends meet, for which he had donated the land. The story that gets me to chuckle the most is Jefferson Davis, the master of a cotton plantation and 179 slaves before the Civil War. At the war's conclusion, he was so broke that he had to accept gifts of money and food from former slaves.

Today, wealthy individuals' descent into poverty is of epic proportions. In 2008, the global financial crisis caused billionaires around the globe to take a huge hit. In Iceland, Bjorgolfur Gudmundsson's net worth was $1.1 billion, but later that same year, he was worth exactly nada, and was later sent to serve 12 months in prison for fraud and embezzlement. Sean Quinn was the richest person in Ireland around the same time as Gudmundsson, with a net worth of about $6 billion. Three years later, he too filed for bankruptcy. Going to South America, add to this pile the Brazilian mining, oil and gas magnate Eike Batista, whose fortune of more than $30 billion evaporated between March 2012 and January 2014.

Don't cry for these former billionaires I mentioned. Their prison uniforms are a clear indication of how they accumulated wealth. The accounts of the rise and fall of their fortunes, pales in comparison to innovative people like Selfridge, who was booted out of the very organization that he created. To veer off at a tangent for a moment, take a minute and imagine that among those outrageous stories of rapid wealth accumulation and subsequent bankruptcy claims, there are families of

white and blue collar employees whose lives were
shredded to pieces.

Keep in mind, bottom line, what I have to emphasize
it that the economic cannibalism system isn't merciful
towards moneyers as well as the poor.

"When so many scholars in the world are calculating, is
it not right that some, who can, dream?"

René Thom

There are a lot of reasons for me to be yelling and
cursing in my sleep. Let me sound the alarm; if one day
the Australian-American business magnate Rupert
Murdoch, decides to capitalize on the intransigence of
economists around the planet to develop a television
show that captures ridiculous cheap shots, it will get the
Kardashians' show canceled. Nowadays, it has become
customary for prodigal mathematicians to flex their
'athleticism' that amounts to careless overindulgence of
brainpower and waste of prospects, resulting in theories
far from the present reality to be celebrated as a
scientific advancement and awarded coveted prizes.
Thomas Piketty might win a Nobel Prize after all, but
his infantile solution to the serious wealth and income
inequality has quashed the significance of the facts he
stitched together. Humanity enslaved and depraved is
no longer capable of retracing Capitalism steps or
renouncing disastrous standard living, bringing itself to
the brink of ruin. To the economic druids; where is the
common sense of the Walrasian and Marshallian
derivative in economic analysis? And to the lecturers,

who recognize the absurdity of using this mathematical approach to dissect market interactions and still have the audacity to quiz their students on its applications, should be guillotined.

What is there to say about the current two party recompense system? I advise friends, acquaintances, and foes not to waste a second on the impotent protest of blue collar pay, as it is currently framed. The fight to raise the minimum wage does nothing more than to cement the idea that the neurons of 'those people' (the term used by my now repentant brother Michel), who organize the merchandise on Walmart's racks or 'those people' who package and serve you the fried delicacies one enjoys in a fast food joint, are only deserving of the minimum of nutrients because their work cannot possibly equate to the brain power required to work at the administrative level of an establishment. The futile wage debate takes the attention away from the hyperbolic sympathy and pampering customs built to 'nourish' the officers, board members, and shareholders of current corporations.

The explosion of millionaires and billionaires in China and the fact that Luanda, the capital of Angola, overtook Tokyo Japan as the most expensive city in the world are rightfully accredited to the dominant form of *conmerce* and *threat*. In the time of prosperity, Capitalism is the best system of wealth accumulation for profiteers, entrepreneurs, and politicians, to make it possible for these gangs to spare residuals on the middle class, while they in turn blind and bind the masses. Yet do I really have to tell you what happens when the pirates' bounty starts to shrink? It is called "company restructuration." The first time I heard this term, I naively thought that every job position would remain intact, and laborers would simply be shifted around, as the term seems to apply. The terrible truth is, laborers are thrown overboard into the unemployment sea and into the jaws of quick loan services and pawn stores.

If this is starting to sound to you as an act of capitulation then you are a horrible reader. Adam Smith and his comrades romanticized the bourgeois landowner's misdeed of regarding and exploiting fellow human beings as dispensable tools by relegating their skillset to one of production inputs. This view still reigns supreme on how our society regards the labor workforce. I shall ask the reader, who are you more thankful for when you pull the plug on your grandmother? Moneyers, who finance the imposing building and the ground-breaking technology? Or medical professionals, who have exhausted their time to extend her life? Let me give you my correct answer; both equally. Surprised? All along, you probably assumed that I was one of those irrational free-market antagonists. Hold your disappointment or joy for a moment there because you might just be right. Please relax, and if you can, hold back your tears of frustration and detach your clenched fingers from your scalp. You are about to experience the most thrilling parapsychological show of your lifetime.

XIII

Abracadabra

"If you would be a real seeker after truth, it is
necessary that at least once in your life you
doubt, as far as possible, all things."
Rene Descartes

On the Sabbath, I generally spend time reviewing
my weekly memory tape and forthrightly rating
every action and moment I've experienced.
Whether you agree or not, the world wouldn't tip to the
brink of collapse if everyone humbly adopted the same
method. The benefits of self-retrospection, and
challenging our previous actions and thoughts, are far
from toning down the tenacity with one state opinions,
rather, when it is deemed critical, at recalibrating one's
arguments. Let's take on the preceding chapter. I swung
an iron bat on Adam Smith's legacy, as if it was a piñata
with a swastika sign or he was the pre-incarnation of the
Fuhrer. As a diehard relativist, I sure sounded totally
like a rude absolutist. Still, I reserve the right to act as a
son of a bitch, without adding the contextual element to
the preceding frame then adding the compass to this
chapter and delightfully elevating the debate.

To put Adam Smith's mind and period in perspective, the sheer volume of The Wealth of Nations is a sign that it was intended to be a history book and couldn't be about Capitalism, as it didn't exist yet. Smith lived around the time where the world was clogged with evidences based on factual ignorance and in England, where a small class of white people felt infinitely superior to other white people and not to say, other races. Yet without drilling deeper to the magmatic center of Smith's blend, these factors don't completely elucidate Smith's wage classification that masks the emasculation and dehumanization of the laboring class, the same faux-pas of blind ideologues.

I am now able to look at myself in the mirror and not feel ashamed. It shouldn't be the case for I have no respect for Marxists and Marxian's, who emphatically refuse to admit that their marvelous creator had highly contributed to the debauchery of economic analysis by calling wage as an advance given to landless people. Then again, this view reflects Marx and Smith's era or a near representation of reality at the time. The same is to say about Michał Kalecki's time, where his model is a mixed bag of two fierce enemies, Marx and Keynes; his central argument is that profiteers are responsible for the dough, whereas the laboring class is depicted as impulsive consumers. And let me assure you, jumping further to Karl Marx's exploitation of labor theory or the Kaleckian model would only add to the general public's confusion and anger. I am also baffled by post Keynes economists, who are still building their line of attack and models on a false premise based on the lampooning of the laboring class.

I can see why Nassau Senior, Adam Smith, Karl
Marx, and Michał Kalecki, to name a few of the
lumpenintelligentsias, have come out with these
offensive model concepts that perpetuated economic
cannibalism. They are a product of a certain era and
time. Yet, they still need to be accountable for what they
have done to our souls, by tipping the power dynamic
towards the side of the profiteers, a concept still
prevailing over the reticent economic scholars.

Charles Goodyear, inventor of vulcanized rubber and
Gridley Bryant, who invented the railway carriage, died
in destitute conditions. It is wrong to think that most of
these inventors lacked the knowledge to broker the right
business deal for themselves. Horrifying flashes I get
from banging on social normality and my conscience is
the pillar of my cynicism. If it looks like a duck, swims
like a duck, and quacks like a duck, it might still not be
a duck; rather, it is a clever trap. Haven't you gotten the
sense that I doubt nearly anything and everything? But
if there is one thing I am sure about, it is my
generation's ability to fix this socio-economic mess.

Around the globe, television news have been filled
with haunting pictures of starving children in Niger, the
boiling anger of Ku Klux Klan directed toward
immigrants, ruthless gangs of El Salvador, Myanmar
insurgencies, and the list goes on and on. Even though
these petrifying social plights result from the inherent
capitalist lopsided mechanism of wealth accumulation, I
was just as sickened as you should be, that there is no
straight remedy. To find a remedy, I had to travel back

in time to find the two keys needed to unleash a new mindset.

> "You never change things by fighting the existing reality. To change something, build a new model that makes the existing model obsolete."
>
> R. Buckminster Fuller

I spent five years in a Jesuit catholic boarding school, where we were all required take an annual bible study course. No one mentioned the story of Lilith, the first woman who was created by God, at the same time and from the same earth as Adam. She was booted out of the Garden of Eden for refusing to lie beneath Adam during sexual intercourse. Then came Eve, who was created from one of Adam's ribs. She succumbs to the serpent's temptation, and ate the forbidden fruit from the tree of the knowledge of good and evil to improve on the way God had made her, and to become all knowing; she shared the fruit with Adam. God furiously kicked out the dissident beings from the Garden of Eden, and their offspring inherited their curse for generations to come. One can find similar mythical tales of the origin of the human species in every civilization; the same figures mentioned are found in the book of Genesis, in the Hebrew Bible, and in Islamic tradition. Is this what is happening to commerce and trade? If feudalism is Lilith, then Capitalism is Eve. The pillar of Capitalism, The United States, got tricked by monetarists to bite on fiat money, the forbidden fruit which opened the gate of hell, the accumulation of debt liabilities surpassing the nation worth, and the rest of the world soon followed. Is this the end of our existence?

There is a fascination with the secrecy behind Freemasonry, based on their 'reportedly' spooky rituals. As the legend of one of their rituals goes, the Third Degree, the candidate portrays Hiram Abiff in the ceremony. Hiram Abiff is fabled as the Grand Master at the building of Solomon's temple, who held the secrets of a Master Mason and earned wages far higher than other laborers. Three disgruntled mason laborers (Jubela, Jubelo and Jubelum), accosted Hiram and demanded the secrets of a Master Mason: "Your life, or the secrets," they threatened. Hiram responded, "My life you can have, my integrity - never." When they failed to extract the secrets from Hiram Abiff, they killed him. Hiram willingly laid down his life rather than betray the trust of the Master Mason. When the criminals were captured and sentenced to death, Jubela's wish was that his throat be cut across and his tongue torn out; Jubelo wanted his left breast torn open and his heart fed to vultures; whilst Jubelum asked for his body severed, and his bowels burnt to ashes and scattered to the four winds of heaven. King Solomon, duly obliged. Ever since, these utterances have been recalled by Freemasons in the penalties prescribed for the breaking of their oaths.

This dramatic scene, is the first step in highlighting that Capitalism wa built on people being part of the guild system in which a limited number of individuals own the means of "production"; there was a tightly controlled, small number of apprentices, and the rest were the illiterate main d'oeuvre. And in this viciously

impenetrable cycle, even apprentices had to agree
working for long periods at low wages, because
employers understood that the skills trade is a mean of
"production" and also a threat to their control over labor.

I am depressed that Adam Smith's vulgar
classification of wage and Nassau Senior's shenanigans,
still have a firm hold on modern innovation and social
progress. The precursor of Capitalism was a structure
where families exchanged their own crop surpluses for
other commodities. How did we get to the self-
enslavement cycle that we know of today? Well, the
response has to do with the origin of wage and how it
was viewed. This quest should transport your
imagination to middle-ages when Flanders was a center
for textiles. As the Flanders got squeezed by Palestine's
increasing wool prices, they turned to their English
neighbors. Guess what? English feudal lords saw in the
Flanders, an appetite for wool as an opportunity to
accumulate immense wealth. This greed kick started the
appropriation avalanches of peasant lands, converting
entire depopulated villages into sheep runs. Don't think
for a minute that the long lasting effect on humanity of
the peasants' dispossession of the means to grow their
own food was the dissolution of poor English social-
economic safety net. Rather, please highlight with a red
marker that this wicked chokehold of the English
peasantry, assembled a class of people at the mercy of
moneyers, who at that time, owned the means of
"production" while this burgeoning 'labor class' had to
survive by working for wages. And this is the second
signature mark of Capitalism.

What is the juice coming out of this mixture? Adam Smith was devilishly right on his perception of wage as Hitler's folly flourished from the imposed socio-economic devastation of Germany after World War I. It's worth noting that contrary to Adam Smith's naïve prediction, moneyers in cahoots with landowners, steadily reduced the pay doled out to the working class, making it impossible for the poor to go back to peasant farming, or to become independent.

What has changed since then? All over the globe, profiteers' (moneyers and landowners) greed has overtaken academia and in pursuit of more wealth they accidently opened up to the laboring class access to higher learning and professional training for the laboring classes. Furthermore, competition has forced them to develop an academic pluralist system, a number of departments and majors that were imaginable decades ago. This revolution on its own, pulled the cap off relic taboos and has been a pivotal game changer. For example, an aspiring physician has to pay for medical training, and goes through years of hazing, residency programs and exams to qualify as a family doctor, a skill once reserved for the few of the 'right' pedigree, or an anesthetist, a field that didn't exist not long ago. I for one, have been on both sides of the hiring process called interviewing. I can testify that it is no secret what potential job and responsibility someone can attain with a gumbo of degrees, training, and experience, because companies are doing their hiring based on defined criteria.

Stepping back to my example of you pulling the plug on your grandmother, I would advise you to send a big thank you card to the big bucks behind the infrastructure, medical providers, and janitors in the medical center. Every party played a critical role in fooling you during the magic trick. If you still can't catch the signal amongst the assortment of bass infused clarinet sounds, I am declaring that neither moneyers, landowners, nor laborers create and sustain jobs; consumers do! To this claim, there is always more than one person in the room, who bitterly points out this premise's entanglement. We are all in fact, customers but then they rush into the boring divertive debate on taxes, regulations, and class warfare. Would you punch me in the face if I say that I don't give a shit if companies provide healthcare benefits to employees? I really don't. Not only do I not shy away from calling out the debate centered around increasing minimum wage nonsense, I insist to campaign that family, friends, and foes not to waste a second on this matter. It is one of several ploys engaged by the self-preserving to pacify social uprisings. And there is no need for entertaining mind-bending mathematical explanations to sort out moneyers, landowners, and laborers in the consumer pot, because it is not the root of our current socio-economic cancer.

Let's say a gentleman hires you to tend to his two cows for a gallon of milk per week. After ten years, the number of his bovines has multiplied by ten. Using the excess bulls, the increased milk production, and the dairy-producer's subsidies, he bought a tractor to expand activities in his farm. By then you, the hired help, got

married, had children, and now have five people to keep
alive on the same pay. If this disproportional
distribution of surplus is replicated in the entire
community, a small passive group would be
accumulating the cheese (literally), while the rest would
be actively propelling the dispiriting gap. This unbalance
is not reasonable for those at the bottom and sustainable
for those on the top because of the inevitable class
dissatisfaction outbursts such as that experienced in
Libya under Muammar Gaddafi, which has since turned
into an unimaginable nightmare. Forget about the
scheme of adding now and then, an ounce of milk
increase in pay or the healthcare benefits that would
patch-up laborers to keep them on task inaudibly, sticks
the bill to the entire community. "Then what is the
solution?" I bet that's what you are shouting. My
answer: To rethink the way we deliberate classes'
recompense system with respect of the natural duality
between moneyers, landowners, and laborers.

Take a thirty second pause, and when you finally
wrap your mind around the contextual and factual
difference between Capitalism's properties and the
twenty-first century reality, even your arrogance
shouldn't hold you back from agreeing with the
undisputable fact that we now buy and own our
individual means of to engage, to participate, or to get
involved in an enterprise. What am I signifying?
Whether you are burning your lungs in a Turkish coal
mine, you land a job as a customer service
representative in India, or a crooked tax collector in
Honduras, you have decided to tie in your means of

engagement, participation, or involvement in an enterprise. Therefore, the risk of failure in such an enterprise, is justly shared throughout its spectrums. It's more apparent when a business closes, moneyers are not the only one to take a hit; employees who had taken the risk of working for this business rather than another are thrown back onto the unemployment line.

You should be now nodding your heads in agreement that we own our means of engagement, participation, or involvement, and the risks are shared by moneyers, landowners, and laborers alike. Therefore, every party's recompense should be based on a percentage of the markup which I will call, from now on, surplus.

I would like to take immense credit for this vision, but the idea of perceiving a percentage is not at a novelty. The approach shouldn't be foreign to you either, it is called in the sales industry commission. Check out government taxes; their rates are in percentages. What I say, if it is good for some sectors and governments, it should be good for all of us. Are you thinking that I am out of my mind adding a fluctuation which could be perceived as an extra headache, to a fast-food restaurant or to Mom-and-Pop enterprises in figuring out their employees' paycheck? But this is where the marvels of human drive to invent and to push technologic boundaries beyond common mortals' imaginations come into play. If you run to your backyard right now, you would be able to catch Joseph Alois Schumpeter, riding butt naked on a white horse. This shouldn't be hard to figure out, if someone can produce a machine that guided spot-on, a missile to an "insurgent's" tent in the middle of nowhere (which generally misses him, but kills

his innocent wives and children), why wouldn't it
calculate to the dime, a McDonalds employee's bi-weekly
paycheck? Then again, the short-term annoyance that
may be felt in doing the right thing, will redefine and
revitalize many industries, including accountants.

This revolution reshapes the aging wealth
distribution and accumulation debate. More importantly,
the fluctuation of labor recompense and the nonissue of
price springiness which we come to expect, deflates class
conflicts. This change is a fictional hecatomb for
moneyers because more money spread around would
incite investment and growth, but it's a true nightmare
for lazy economists because it ejects all the outmoded
theories (e.g. market clearing) that they cling to today.

> "Taking a new step, uttering a new word, is
> what people fear most."
> Fyodor Dostoyevsky

My wife and I have recently been introduced to a really
funny guy who has pancreatic cancer. What a time to
jump into someone's life, I thought. As I watched with a
skeptic eye, family and friends clamoring around him, it
felt like people were selfishly reminding him that his life
was fading away. Ironically, one or two folks that he
knew, who thought to be in better shape than he was,
went kaput before him. Now before you think that I am
the worst person who has ever written a book, I have
justifiable reasons for being appalled by the morbid
masquerade. Tara lost her mother to breast cancer. I
had to watch my father's serpentine smile fade away and

turn into the most caring man in the Universe; unfortunately he returned to himself when he overcame cancer. I am used to the unenlightened group, chanting out loud that there are lessons learned from witnessing a friend or a family member facing death; and that every moment in life counts. You have to be a douchebag not to know that life is an experience and not an art. To be fair, I was not long ago one of those morons. And you probably still are! I know that I have done more than I should have when I wasn't afraid to fail, to live. Now that the signal is sounding clearer, I have gone all the way down my bucket list, but now I am stuck on this final challenge, and I need you.

I see Capitalism as the lady in the quest for looking eternally young and attractive to the eyes of her manifold schizophrenic boyfriends. Despite countless boob jobs, tanning bed overuse, and expensive Botox injections, instead of a youthful appearance, she looks monstrously creepier. To her luck, none of her boyfriends can notice her severely sunburned legs, because they are hooked on the pipe. Any capitalist fanatics, please chill out! A new economic form doesn't automatically render your cheered antique system obsolete, but provides an alternative (wink wink). Let's cut the bull here, we cannot stubbornly ride Capitalism's cataclysmically prone ferry forever.

Why don't we have a real full bodied alternative system to Capitalism? Well, a lot of cancer patients are unaware of other treatments than the conventional trinity of painful surgery, radiation, and chemotherapy. And today, a parallel ignorance exists in commerce (I have intentionally chopped off "and trade"). Now and then, I have used the terms business, entrepreneur, firm, Gross Domestic Product, production industry, service industry, monopoly, and other capitalistic lingo which are facets of corporatism to spare the reader of any headache and avoid getting you guys lost in my mind's labyrinth. I used these terminologies because they are so embedded in the global culture. The word 'trade' is as laughable as bartering because no one, and no nation, trades. We now make, sell, and buy. And when you think of the billions of dollars spent around the globe on marketing schemes and product research and development, it disputes the notion that the goal of a business is only to maximize profit for its shareholders. Rather, it cements the idea that the primary goal, is to break potential customers' indifference.

Okay readers, the foremost challenges facing first, second and third world nations, is none other than blue and white collar laborers meager recompense and wealth distribution in its entirety. I know, you're probably pissed off that I messed with your minds a little on Hop O' my thumb, for letting you believe that I agreed with the mainstream diagnosis of the ailing developing nations and for prescribing a placebo for development. I am sorry. Would you have sincerely kept reading this book if I told you the right remedy to every nations' *casse-tête chinois*? I don't think so. The real solution is to grasp the new global trend and understand *Ethosism*. This paradigm transcends traditional boundaries.

Unquestionably, higher learning is vital to progress, but it can only go so far at expanding a citizen's aspirations. A strong commitment to education by itself, cannot help poor nations to catch up with the current world's most innovative economies. Today, their few intellectuals of any significant caliber are essentially high priests, at the service of paranoid pharaohs. What is the key to impoverished countries having an opportunity to leapfrog with the rest of the developing world, which in turn is ultimately beneficial to developed nations? It is not democracy. It is intellectual freedom (political freedom is a tiny part of it) that leads to the adoption of an innovative enterprise culture. Only then these faltering nations could properly promote highly specialized small and medium-sized enterprises.

You and I have been through the good and bad, and I am really surprised that you have hung on. Bravo! But let us take this abstract relationship to the next level of trust. At the outset of this new journey, I will put an end to the sarcasm and push corporatism's terms over our memories' cliff. All over the world, young and old folks have a general sense today, that a costly higher learning degree doesn't mean anything anymore. That sense is false. Instead, I point out that Capitalism wasn't built for a large number of individuals owning *means of engagement, participation, or involvement*, which is the twenty-first century global reality.

The supremacy of Capitalism is due to the fact that it was a reality that mirrors social norms and capital centered dynamism arising out of feudalism (I don't consider Mercantilism). As I already explained, it was noticed by Adam Smith, and well recorded by Karl Marx in (by the way, Karl Marx was the second person who coined the term Capitalism). Whereas Socialism and

Communism, spirited economic insurgency movements, failed because they were both manufactured human centered models imposed upon deeply rooted capitalistic societies. In the eighteenth century, Capitalism chased away feudalism and has since effortlessly engulfed the majority of the world. New social norms and human centered reality are emerging; but we have yet to realize that the twenty-first century is spearheading a stronger global drive, Ethosism, that is fluently kicking Capitalism's butt, and setting us free.

I enjoy that today's corporatism is more and more looking like a mirage, the old way to maneuver around commerce trails that grants full power to profiteers to belittle other players. The number of private groups ready to send a satellite and tourists into space, beating every advanced nations' space programs, is a clear indication that the organizational structure relevant to the twenty-first century and chasing out Capitalism dinosaurs are enterprises. *Enterprise* is the key term I am going to use to spearhead the rest of this book.

A precursor story is when IBM was looking for a business and hara-kiri, Apple, and Microsoft saw an enterprise and sprung out billionaires. And now Chinese teenagers are making knockoff Nokias from the vast component bazaars of Shenzhen and putting giant cellular phone makers on a panic mode. The global trend put anyone in Mozambique with the guts to write a novel a click away to conquer the e-book world. It has been announced that there will soon be a kit available to print out a gun or a DNA sequence in the comfort of your own home. What about ordering your company logo from a freelance artist in Pakistan on Fiverr.com and get it the next day for a fraction of what it would cost you to wait for the overpriced and overrated Vignellis to quit arguing between themselves? Have you watched the video of Saith Shahid Nazir (One pound fish man)? Can you dance like the ghetto kids? In Uganda, a math teacher put a video on YouTube of kids dancing on a street turning them in to an instant national and international sensation and made these kids and families future a little less grimmer.

Have you booked a room using Airbnb or hailed a ride using Uber services? Used Couchsurfing.org in Latin America? Do you own a bitcoin? Bought anything on Alibaba.com? Purchased this book online? If your answer is no to every one of these questions then you must still be dancing to Abba beats or shaking your scantily clad rear in a remote Amazonian tribe. For the rest of you, you have a sense of enterprises coalescing individuals' means of participation or engagement to break customers' indifference towards their products or services. As you and I are sharing the same planet right now, we should have a common belief that commerce mammoths who are centered on corporatism models are dying and are being overtaken by enterprises. There is an exhilaration felt after experiencing this thrilling *open interactions*. It should be clear to you that in this *Ethosism* form of economy, currently normalizing how market agents mingle, and the relics of Capitalism *free market* are downright toxic. If you just missed it, I used the term interaction instead of market, the latter has long ceased to exist.

Once again, I will take the time to bellow loud and clear to your conscience that every agent in an enterprise carries a heavily weighted risk by tying down their individual means of engagement, participation, or involvement. And there are plenty of signs that young ethosists *conceptors, conductors,* and *curators,* are adjusting to this seemingly chaotic reality. The fact that now a commerce's actions are essentially a collage of individual means, and the existence of the sacrosanct natural duality between laborers, landowners, and moneyers, a nominal weighted recompense of any party doesn't make any sense. It is justly right that for every agent in an enterprise, recompense is a negotiated percentage of the surplus (mark-up). New ethosists from Silicon Valley to rural Malawi, successes are fundamentally based on the participation or engagement of agents in the form of labor, concept, or dough. Twenty-first century enterprise's conceptors and conductors ingenuously avoid the *patent and start-up fund trap* that made a genius like Walter Shaw die penniless by self-reliance or group-reliance.

In the dissection of the new form of making, selling, and buying products and services, Ethosism, enterprises are led by *revenue, profit,* and *wage,* which is distinct from Capitalism industry components, *production* and *service.* You must be asking, what the hell I am talking about! Let me walk you slowly through this chaotic and brave new world.

Revenue led enterprises consist of making an object, in its most simplistic form; these are activities that lead to an output. And this is whether the output is a chair or a computer software. A surplus, revenue, is derived from a just price or cost of extracting and/or modifying of one or more material(s) with the active engagement of laborers with the either passive or active engagement of moneyers and the either passive or active engagement of landowners to bring either passive or active conceptors ideas to life.

Profit led enterprises orbit around production's output and are divided into sales, the selling of an object, and service, maintaining or delivery of an object. A surplus, profit, is derived from a fluctuant market price (bouncing from the just price up to the natural price) of auctioning off one or combined two or more output(s) without altering its (their) substance with the active participation of laborers and with the either passive or active participation of moneyers and the either passive or active participation of landowners to bring either passive or active conductors ideas to life. When I say these activities don't totally alter the substance of the output, I see the example of a restaurant patron's plate of food. The baby-back ribs are not legally killed in the kitchen, nor pulled from the restaurant's backyard; there is a division.

The last nugget of Ethosism, is that wage or non-profit based enterprises are public services and charities. These enterprises generate a *surplus,* contributions (e.g. taxes) or donations (e.g. charity), directly from the active involvement of laborers and

passive or active curators to bring one or more either
passive or active societies initiatives to life.
What is the difference between a conceptor, a conductor,
and a curator? A conceptor's ideas are protected by a
patent whereas a conductor's idea is trademarked. A
curator is a custodian of the public's welfare. Judging by
western government's pragmatism and aggressive
promotion of their home countries, aren't governments
mutating into *too big to fail* citizen enterprises?
To summarize this passage:

> Revenue enterprise generates surplus by the
> engagement of parties' means; therefore, all the
> engaged parties' recompense should be in
> percentage of the revenue.
>
> Profit enterprise generates surplus by the
> participation of parties' means; therefore all the
> participating parties' recompense should be in
> percentage of the profit.
>
> Non-profit enterprises, generate a surplus by the
> involvement of parties' means; however, all the
> parties involved recompense should be a fixed
> wage because the aim in the public sector is not to
> generate a surplus for any party involved in this
> enterprise, but rather, for the general public
> welfare programs such as building roads,
> maintaining a standing military force, or assisting
> the less fortunate.

Still, this global new order needs a couple more
ingredients to be treated as an alternative to Capitalism
and adopted by institutions (please do). There is no

doubt to become the answer to socio-economic dissatisfaction, it needs to completely do away with the huge cat and tiny mouse game between lucrative percentage return on investment and pintsized nominal wages. It requires a demarcation line to be drawn between sectors. Enterprises should be restricted to either (1) revenue based, (2) profit based, or (3) non-profit based.

Have you realized that I haven't wrote much about the Internet? Well, its role in the global revolution is exaggerated. By no means am I trying to diminish the internet factor, but this communication innovation is not the soul of the new economic era and interactions, rather it brought transparency that have cemented Ethosism's presence.

"The snake which cannot cast its skin has to die. As well the minds which are prevented from changing their opinions; they cease to be mind."

Friedrich Nietzsche

I traced my childhood obsession with alchemy, as it was told in the Middles Ages, as the key in turning ordinary rock into gold. My goal of stacking up this shining metal was not for its shiny exterior but to buy a new planet for the poor and abused children. I had the same hope when I took on economics, but like alchemy, it has become a mixture of white magic and unsubstantiated theories flavored with much superstition. There are parallel lines that can be easily drawn between alchemy and economics. Alchemists' efforts were largely misdirected by classical Greek philosophers who argued that all substances were made up of four basic elements: air, earth, fire, and water. Economists argue that all markets are made up of four basic elements as well: price, quantity, demand, and supply.

It took a skeptic chemist like Antoine-Laurent Lavoisier, whose theory of combustion detected oxygen and claiming chemical reactions that take place during respiration in animals is the same as combustion. In fact, he buried once and for all alchemy and its useless hunt. I don't get the same salvation sign when I visit colleges and universities' economic departments across both hemispheres. I find angry delusional old men filling the heads of kids (pure asshole parrots), with pure garbage. The incoherence in the entire economic scholastic regime call in question the entire framework of theories and social remedies birth of out them that dominate everyday life. The tumbling and rumbling by itself demystifies the ideology of economic academia divination.

In a world where diminishing return is used instead of collapse, you can understand well how marginal utility consumption is twisted. Why are we all not comfortable when giving an additional apple or taking an additional dollar away, has nothing to do with happiness; rather, the perishability of these two commodities. If you have a stomach like mine, you get full on one apple. The more apples you get, you are faced with the guilt of glut or waste. Wealth accumulation primer is greed; somebody with ten dollars in their pocket knows there is less you can do with it and in turn, it is easier for them to give a dollar away. Compared to a billionaire, to whom losing a dollar will take him/her away from the high class of billionaire status. What am I screaming out here? Marginal utility is equal to moral cost, which is guilt or deprivation.

The economic faculty bench of is not only filled with old white males with bad teeth, and old, funny talking Indians. In these *madrassas*, I have run into intellectual Siamese midgets, Chinese, angry black American women, sexual predator Africans- all spitting out sermons from the same satanic verses. Where alchemists failed, economists have until now, partially succeeded in concocting an elixir of life that would make them live forever; it is true that when you check that long after Hicks's recantation of the temporary general equilibrium method, uncertainty has become improbable, general equilibrium and marginalism still reigns supreme over economics.

> "Give me liberty, or give me death!"
> Patrick Henry

I have harshly criticized the new rat pack of anointed economists, because of their failure to properly address global inequality by restricting the discussion to distributive issues in the context of moneyers' interest groups. These so-called scholars' beautifully depicted spreadsheets just prove that Capitalism is doing exactly what it was supposed to do; create surplus and confine immense wealth into the hands of a small class of ruthless profiteers. Don't be fooled by their tales and explanations which has fundamentally erroneous assumptions or by their crocodile tears.

The dictatorial way economics is taught in orthodox institutions, is in comparison, not worse than the indoctrination and hazing in the few surviving heterox programs. For someone who has been lashed to the mast by both sides, I can testify that you lose the will of rebelling against the status quo. Theses masters of mass manipulation obscure logical fallacies and inconsistencies to entrench bling supporters and brown-nosers into the two camps and watch them battle it out to the death. I say no to this meaningless gladiators cage fight to please these self-professed Caesars; we are in dear need of a new discipline.

It is hard to gain scholastic virtuous in a field where manufacturing rubbish insane justification is cost-efficiency, enterprise blunder is painted as diminishing return, and environmentalists orate days and nights out sustainability while turning a blind eye on overconsumption. What if we abandon the idea of rethinking economics and get rid of it all together? We have sufficient power to create this change. Economy is plagued with stupid cacophony. Let us together do a good thing to humanity and start fresh with a quantum paradigm study to the way we make, sell, and buy (erase the word commerce in your mind) before you and I get cast away, far away!

Sky High

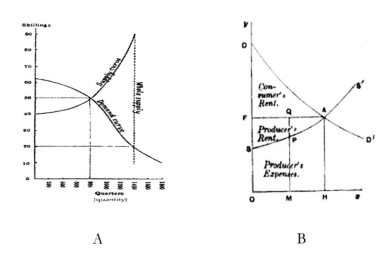

A   B

If I do ask you, what is the difference between the
Graphic Representation of the Laws of Supply and
Demand A and B? Well as you can see nothing
much. After climbing on Antoine-Augustin Cournot, Karl
Rau, Jules Dupuit, and Hans von Mangoldt, sadly
Marshall and his cadets still have the audacity to deny
the merit to Fleeming Jenkin, who employed the cross
diagram in print in 1870 before Marshall published it in
his Pure Theory of Domestic Values (1879) and later in
his Principles of Economics (1890). More shocking is the
number of concepts (price elasticity of demand and

supply, of stability of equilibrium, of the possibility of multiple equilibria, of comparative statics analyses involving shifts in the curves, of consumers' and producers' surplus, of constant, increasing and decreasing costs, of pricing of joint and composite products, of potential benefits of price discrimination, of tax incidence analysis, of deadweight welfare loss triangles and the allocative inefficiency of monopoly) that are attributed to Marshall or his greatest impersonators. You and I are not going to spend time on this controversy because classical graphs rightfully depicted capitalisms' simplicity during their time. Yet these notions have engulfed generations of Marshall's offspring to the obsession of market clearing; in in other words, forcing accidental correlation to plug in an equilibrium in market decomposition. Today, this approach should not reign supreme over our 21st century realities. To that end, I am going to tease your mind with new projections that capture the real world and the current dominant feature of Ethosism, individual interactions.

Rise or Fall

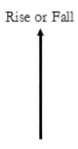

Fig. 1
e.g. Price

Accumulate
value
time

Fig. 2
e.g. commodity

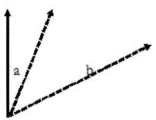

Compare two commodities
a
b

Fig3
a. Diamond
b. Bread

Prices

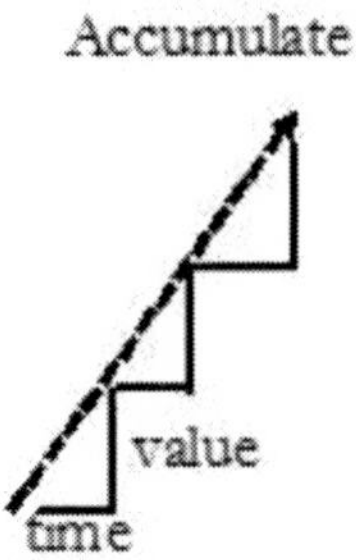

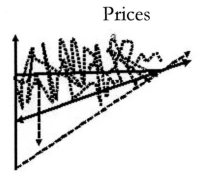

Fig. 4

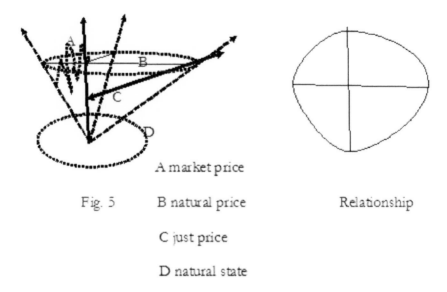

Fig. 5

A market price

B natural price

C just price

D natural state

Relationship

Hospital model

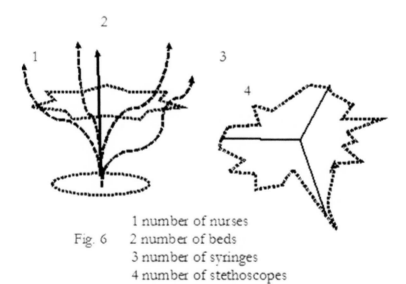

Fig. 6

1 number of nurses
2 number of beds
3 number of syringes
4 number of stethoscopes

Full Circle

At some point of my life I figured out that touring hell is not killing me fast enough, and I decided to go after the most prominent goal of my life: making a positive difference. Far from trying to sway the future or consumed in the goal of writing a masterpiece, this book is an attempt to affect the moment and to crank up readers' brains.

I couldn't finish this book without completely cleaning up my closet, not of course totally in Eminem style. In the exercise of writing this book, I have battled my fear and ego. To my surprise, I rode this wild rollercoaster to end up where I have unintentionally begun; in the lives of people that are truly dear to me. As I am pouring every one of these lines straight from my blotted heart, I can't help by breakdown all in tears!!!

Dear Bidetty (my mom): My plan is to show you that I understand.

Hello Claudine: Ain't a woman alive or dead that could take your place!!!

Wazzup Betty: There's no way I can pay you back

Hey Gaga: Keep your head up

Chris and Mathias: I hope that you would one day find a way to forgive me

Le vieux (my dad) : Sing with me What's going on

And finally Tara (Mere ya Palais): You are appreciated

Notes

Abuse, Poverty and Migration: Investigating Migrants' Motivations to Leave Home in Burma. Tak?: Karen Human Rights Group, 2009.

Allen, Robert C. The British Industrial Revolution in Global Perspective. Cambridge: Cambridge University Press, 2009.

Alter, Shannon. "Marketing, Gangnam Style: Making a First Impression before Your First Impression." Journal of Property Management, January 1, 2013.

Andrews, V. C. Twisted Roots. New York: Pocket Books, 2002.

Anzovin, Steven. South Africa: Apartheid and Divestiture. New York: H.W. Wilson, 1987.

AP Exclusive: Bangladesh Factory Flaws Highlighted." AP Online, June 13, 2013. Accessed September 24, 2014. http://www.highbeam.com/doc/1A1-231667d321bf44a09dd2b240439fbbca.html?

"Arab Spring a Call for Dignity, Justice and Freedom, Says King." Jordan News Agency, March 3, 2012.

"Arab Spring Shakes up Regional Power Balance." The Daily Star (Beirut, Lebanon), December 28, 2011. Accessed February 24, 2014. http://www.highbeam.com/doc/1G1-275823075.html?

Bacon, Charley Arthur. The Abstinence Theory of Nassau Senior and Its Critique by Eugen Von Bohm Bawerk. 1992.

Barwah, Mahama. The Effect of IMF Programs in Sub Sahara Africa: Does IMF Intervention Achieve Macroeconomic Stability and Economic Growth? The Case for Sub-Sahara Africa. Saarbrücken: LAP Lambert Academic Publishing, 2011.

Baumgardner, Frank T. Brooks. "Gross Domestic Product by State: Advance Statistics for 2011 and Revised Statistics for 1997-2010." Survey of Current Business, July 1, 2012.

Bawerk, Eugen Von. Capital and Interest. South Holland, Ill.: Libertarian Press, 1959.

Bernat, J. Christopher. Sleeping Rough in Port-au-Prince an Ethnography of Street Children and Violence in Haiti. Gainesville, FL: University Press of Florida, 2006.

"Best-Selling Author Michelle Alexander and Drug Policy Alliance's Asha Bandele Discuss Impact of the New Jim Crow, and Next Steps to End the Drug War and Mass Incarceration." States News Service, March 4, 2014.

"Big Brands Rejected Bangladesh Factory Safety Plan." AP Worldstream, April 26, 2013.

Blaug, Mark. Who's Who in Economics. 4th ed. Cheltenham, UK: Edward Elgar Pub., 2003.

Blumenthal, Karen. Six Days in October: The Stock Market Crash of 1929. New York, N.Y.: Atheneum Books for Young Readers, 2002.

Boo, Katherine. Behind the Beautiful Forevers: Life, Death, and Hope in a Mumbai Undercity. Brunswick, Vic.: Scribe Publications, 2012.

Borodina, S. D. Investing in BRIC Countries: Evaluating Risk and Governance in Brazil, Russia, India, & China. New York: McGraw-Hill, 2010.

Bourne, Richard. Lula of Brazil: The Story so Far. Berkeley: University of California Press, 2008.

Bowley, Marian. Nassau Senior and classical economics. New York: Octagon Books, 1967.

Brinkley, Douglas. The Great Deluge: Hurricane Katrina, New Orleans, and the Mississippi Gulf Coast. New York: Morrow, 2006.

Bruckberger, R. The Stork and the Jewels,. New York: Harper, 1951.

Chang, Ha. Bad Samaritans: The Myth of Free Trade and the Secret History of Capitalism. New York, NY: Bloomsbury Press, 2008.

Cheah, Joseph, and Grace Ji Kim. Theological Reflections on "Gangnam Style": A Racial, Sexual, and Cultural Critique. New York: Palgrave Macmillan, 2014.

"CIA World Fact book." Central Intelligence Agency. Accessed June 15, 2014. https://www.cia.gov/library/publications/the-world-factbook/rankorder/2004rank.html.

Coleman, William. "Gauging Economic Performance Under Changing Terms Of Trade: Real Gross Domestic Income Or Real Gross Domestic Product?" Economic Papers: A Journal of Applied Economics and Policy: 329-42.

Creedy, John. Demand and Exchange in Economic Analysis: A History from Cournot to Marshall. Aldershot Hants, England: E. Elgar Pub., 1992.

Dongria Tribals Want Vedanta Plant out of Odisha." Headlines Today (New Delhi, India), July 19, 2013.

Drucker, Ernest M. A Plague of Prisons: The Epidemiology of Mass Incarceration in America. New York: New Press :, 2011.

Eichstaedt, Peter H. Consuming the Congo: War and Conflict Minerals in the World's Deadliest Place. Chicago, Ill.: Lawrence Hill Books, 2011.

Ekelund, Robert B., and Robert F. Bert. A History of Economic Theory and Method. New York: McGraw-Hill, 1975.

Falke, Cassandra. Intersections in Christianity and Critical Theory. Basingstoke, Hampshire: Palgrave Macmillan, 2010.

Garnier, Germain. Germain Garnier Correspondence. Oxford: Electronic Enlightenment Project, 2008.

Genius on Hold. Performed by Frank Langella, Walter L. Shaw. 2013. Film.

Gettings, Christine Nicole. Burma's Enigmatic Dictator: The Consolidation of Senior General Than Shwe's Power. 2008.

Goldthorpe, J. E., and J. E. Goldthorpe. The Sociology of Post-colonial Societies: Economic Disparity, Cultural Diversity, and Development. Cambridge: Cambridge University Press, 1996.

Greif, Avner, and Murat Iyigun. What Did the Old Poor Law Really Accomplish? A Redux. Bonn: IZA, 2013.

Grey, Vivian. The Chemist Who Lost His Head: The Story of Antoine Laurent Lavoisier. New York: Coward, McCann & Geoghegan, 1982.

Grovum, Jake. "Another round of Food Stamp Cuts in States." USA Today. March 26, 2014. Accessed July 2, 2014. http://www.usatoday.com/story/news/nation/2014/03/26/stateline-food-stamps-benefits/6906913/.

Heaton, Graham. The Corruption. Gamlingay: Authors OnLine, 2011.

Heo, Uk, and Terence Roehrig. South Korea since 1980. New York: Cambridge University Press, 2010.

Hochschild, Adam. King Leopold's Ghost: A Story of Greed, Terror, and Heroism in Colonial Africa. Boston: Houghton Mifflin, 1998.

India Home to 70 Billionaires; Mukesh Ambani Richest." Daily News (Colombo, Sri Lanka), March 3, 2014. Accessed September 1, 2014 from: http://www.highbeam.com/doc/1G1-360268644.html?

Jaffe, Meryl. Departing The Text Blog, February 3, 2013. Accessed August 11, 2014 from: http://departingthetext.blogspot.com/2013/02/delayed-gratification-and-impulse.html

Jenkin, Fleeming. The Graphic Representation of the Laws of Supply and Demand, and Their Application to Labour. 1870.

Joyce, Peter. Namibia: Land of Contrast. Cape Town: Struik, 1996.

Klitgaard, Robert. "Corruption Can Be Beaten - as Long as Civil Society Rises to the Challenge." Cape Times, March 1, 2010.

Lassalle, Ferdinand, and F. Keddell. What Is Capital? New York: New York Labor News, 1900.

Kuhn, Thomas S. Structure of scientific revolutions. Chicago: University of Chicago Press, 1970

Li, Peilin. Handbook on Social Stratification in the BRIC Countries Change and Perspective. Singapore: World Scientific Publishing Company, 2013.

Madsen, Axel. John Jacob Astor: America's First Multimillionaire. New York: John Wiley, 2001.

Marshall, Alfred, and C. W. Guillebaud. Principles of economics. 9th (variorum) ed. London: Macmillan for the Royal Economic Society, 1961.

Marshall, Alfred. The Pure Theory of Foreign Trade The Pure Theory of Domestic Values. London: London School of Economics and Political Science, 1930.

McElvaine, Robert S. The Great Depression: America, 1929-1941. New York, N.Y.: Times Books, 1984.

Miller, Frederic P. Haitian Revolution: French Colonial Empire, Saint-Domingue. Haitian Vodou, Bois Caiman, Dutty Boukman,

French Revolution, Polish Legions (Napoleonic Period). Beau Bassin, Mauritius: Alphascript Pub.,:, 2009.

Morgan, Giles. Freemasonry. Harpenden: Pocket Essentials, 2007.

Niehans, Ju. A History of Economic Theory: Classic Contributions, 1720-1980. Baltimore: Johns Hopkins University Press, 1990.

Niger : AREVA in Niger: The Group Takes Action for Defamation." Mena Report, December 21, 2012.

Nigeria Digs For Abacha's Plundered Fortune; Ex-Ruler Is Accused Of Stealing Billions." The Washington Post, August 17, 1998.

Ott, Thomas O. The Haitian Revolution, 1789-1804,. Knoxville: University of Tennessee Press, 1973.

Pande, Rekha. Globalization, Technology Diffusion and Gender Disparity: Social Impacts of ICTs. Hershey, PA: Information Science Reference, 2012.

Pelle, Stefano. Understanding Emerging Markets Building Business BRIC by Brick. New Delhi: Response Books ;, 2007.

Piketty, Thomas, and Arthur Goldhammer. Capital in the Twenty-first Century, 2014.

Pound, Reginald. Selfridge: A Biography. London: Heinemann, 1960.

Red Obsession. 2013. Film.

Reisman, George, and George Reisman. Capitalism: a treatise on economics. Ottawa, Ill.: Jameson Books,1996.

Ricardo, David. On the Principles of Political Economy and Taxation. London: Electric Book, 2001.

Robbins, Lionel Robbins. Wages: An Introductory Analysis of the Wage System under Modern Capitalism. London: Jarrolds, 1926.

Rothbard, Murray Newton. An Austrian perspective on the history of economic thought. Aldershot, Hants, England: E. Elgar Pub., 1995.

Rubin, Isaak Il. A history of economic thought. London: Ink Links ;, 1979.

S, Re. Early Developments in Mathematical Economics. London: Macmillan;, 1961.

Salter, Christopher L. South Korea. Philadelphia: Chelsea House Publishers, 2003.

Schwarz, Richard W. Dr. John Harvey Kellogg as a Social Gospel Practitioner. 1964.

Sen, Amartya, and James E. Foster. On Economic Inequality. Enl. ed. Oxford: Clarendon Press ;, 1997.

Senior, Nassau William. Political economy. London: J.J. Griffin, 1850.

Silverstein, Ken. The Secret Life of a Shopaholic: How an African Dictator's Playboy Son Went on a Multi-million Dollar Shopping Spree in the U.S. : A Report. London: Global Witness, 2009.

Schneider, Erich. Hans Von Mangoldt on Price Theory: A Contribution to the History of Mathematical Economics. S.l.: S.n., 1960.

Schumpeter, Joseph A. History of Economic Analysis;. New York: Oxford University Press, 1954.

Schumpeter, Joseph A. Capitalism, Socialism, and Democracy. 3d ed. New York: Harper, 1950.

Smith, Adam. The Wealth of Nations: The Economics Classic : A Selected Edition for the Contemporary Reader. Chichester: Capstone, 2010.

Smith, Anna Marie. Welfare Reform and Sexual Regulation. New York: Cambridge University Press, 2007.

Sothern, Billy. Down in New Orleans Reflections from a Drowned City. Berkeley, Calif.: University of California Press, 2007.

Stearns, Peter N.. Encyclopedia of European social history from 1350 to 2000. Detroit, Mich.: Charles Scribner's Sons, 2001.

Steytler, N. C. The Freedom Charter and Beyond: Founding Principles for a Democratic South African Legal Order. Cape Town: Wyvern, 1991.

Teodorin Obiang Nguema Indicted in Bien Mal Acquis Case." States News Service, March 20, 2014.

The Crowd in History; a Study of Popular Disturbances in France and England, 1730-1848. New York: Wiley, 1964.

The Human Development Cost of the King of Swaziland's Lifestyle and His "Bevy" of Wives." States News Service, September 21, 2012.

Tissot, Simon. L'onanisme: Dissertation Sur Les Maladies Produites Par La Masturbation. S.l.: Saraswati Press, 2012.

Truth and Reconciliation Commission of South Africa Report. Cape Town: Truth and Reconciliation Commission ;, 1999.

Wedeman, Andrew Hall. Double Paradox: Rapid Growth and Rising Corruption in China. Ithaca: Cornell University Press, 2012.

Whately, Richard. Introductory Lectures on Political Economy. New York: A.M. Kelley, 1966.

Williams, Karen Lynn, and Wendy Stone. Beatrice's Dream: A Story of Kibera Slum. London: Frances Lincoln Children's Books, 2011.

Worden, Nigel. The Making of Modern South Africa: Conquest, Segregation, and Apartheid. Oxford: Blackwell, 1994.

Yarber, William L., and Barbara Werner Sayad. Human Sexuality: Diversity in Contemporary America. 8th ed. New York: McGraw-Hill, 2013.

Index

A

academic pluralist system, 189

accumulation of debt liabilities, 186

accuracy, 10

Adam Smith, 110, 117, 121, 137, 155, 157, 167, 168, 169, 171, 181, 183, 184, 185, 188, 189, 197, 219

addiction, 41, 45, 49, 61, 94, 146

Adolf Hitler, 74

African National Congress (ANC), 37

Albert Einstein, 175

Alberto Vilar, 176

alcoholism, 154

Alexander Fleming, 175

Alexander the Great, 172

Alfonso and Jose Fanjul, 61

Alfred Fisher, 121

Alfred Kinsey, 124

Alfred Marshall, 117

Ali Abdullah Saleh, 91

alpha male, 150

alternative, 4, 7, 10, 55, 75, 134, 194

alternative to Capitalism, 4, 202

Amendment of the Poor Law act, 113

American's Abstinence theory, 122

Andre Carnegie, 68

Angola, 177, 180

anti-masturbation food, 123

Antoine-Laurent Lavoisier, 203

Antonio Meucci, 175

Apartheid, 2, 6, 36, 37, 38, 39, 213, 220

Arab Spring, 84, 91, 93, 104, 213

Areva, 51

Argentina, 17, 177

art, 3, 90, 108, 109, 194

Arthur William Cutten, 73

Aryan economic, 122

August Stauch, 136

Aung San Su Kyi, 30

austerity, 21

B

Bangladesh, 48, 49, 50, 152, 213, 214

Bank of America, 173

Barack Obama, 14

Baron Eric de Rothschild, 141

Belgium, 19, 20, 54

Bergdorf Goodman, 25

Bernard Madoff, 176, 177

bifidobacteria, 81

Bill Clinton, 63, 104

Bill Gates, 68, 107

Bin Laden, 45

Bjorgolfur Gudmundsson, 178

black robes, 53

Böhm-Bawerk, 117, 118, 121

Boko Haram, 65

Brazil, 7, 39, 75, 95, 96, 97, 98, 99, 177, 214, 215

BRIC, 7, 14, 95, 214, 217, 218

BRICS, 98

Bulgaria, iii

Burundi, 19, 107

C

capital, iii, 32, 34, 40, 44, 50, 60, 84, 111, 116, 117, 118, 120, 122, 125, 196

capital accumulation, 114, 117, 118, 120, 122, 125

Capitalism, 3, 7, 8, 9, 10, 15, 19, 20, 21, 22, 32, 53, 58, 61, 63, 74, 75, 82, 83, 100, 109, 115, 119, 129, 132, 158, 160, 171, 176, 180, 184, 186, 187, 188, 191, 194, 196, 197, 198, 204

Capitalism in the 21st century, 131

capitalists, 53, 66, 110, 117, 120, 121, 133, 146, 159

Cargill, 97

Catherine the Great of Russia, 70

centralized economies, 20

Chad, 155

Charles Darwin, 172

Charles Goodyear, 185

childhood obesity, 46

China, iii, 7, 14, 21, 44, 95, 97, 98, 99, 131, 177, 180, 214, 220

city of Saint Petersburg, 29

city of Tampa, 28

classical, 5, 18, 108, 110, 121, 157, 171, 203, 215

colonization, 19, 54, 67, 93, 96, 154

Coltan, 55

commerce and trade, 9, 106, 109, 119, 186

Communism, 8, 20, 96, 154, 197

company restructuration, 181

comparative advantage, 19, 156

concept, 10, 67, 111, 115, 117, 118, 146, 185, 199

conceptors, 199, 200

conductors, 199, 200

conmerce and threat, 180

conscienceversion, 129

consciousness, 24, 95, 104

consumerism, 131, 143, 159, 173

consumption, 40, 44, 116, 146

contributions, 61, 92, 118, 157, 200

corporatism, 195, 197, 198

corruptibility, 81, 82

corruption, 14, 33, 50, 80, 81, 82, 132, 154

curators, 199, 201

D

Dambisa Felicia Moyo, 67

Daniel Drew, 177

Das Kapital, 3

David Rockefeller, 68

David Tissot, 122

De Beers, 138

debacle, 91

dehumanization, 184

delusional, 9, 170, 203

demagogues, 116

democracy, 63, 94, 96, 196

Democratic Republic of Congo, ii, 4, 124, 174

Dennis Tito, 125

despair, ii, 18, 95

desperation, 32, 102

Despots grooming, 85

developing countries, 19, 20, 79

development, 14, 15, 16, 19, 58, 68, 81, 93, 117, 195

Dhaka garment factory, 50

diamonds, 29, 83, 137, 138, 139, 147

dictators, 35, 38, 46, 84

dignity, 93, 94

disparity, 4, 6, 8, 27, 94, 106, 133, 156

Donald Trump, 26

donations, 200

Dongria Kondh, 57, 59

Dr. Keith Rowley, 41

duality between labor and profit, 159

Dubai, 85, 149

Dutty Boukman, 103, 217

E

Eastern region of Africa, ii, 14

economic cannibalism, 19, 179, 185

economic crisis, 74, 119

economic development, 94

economic doctrine, 21

economic genocides, 80

economic palliative remedies, 22

Edward Snowden, 89

Egypt, 114, 149, 177

Eike Batista, 178

El Salvador, iii, 177, 185

Elements of Logic, 113

elitist, 106

emasculation, 184

embezzlement, 80, 83, 84, 178

Emperor Xuanzong, 44

engagement, 15, 138, 147, 192, 196, 198, 199, 200, 201

England's Old Poor Law, 109

Enterprise, 197

Ernest Duchesne, 175

Ernesto Che Guevara, 104

Ethiopia, ii, 13, 160

Ethosism, 1, 196, 197, 198, 199, 200, 202

Eve, 36, 140, 186

excess capacity, 20

F

F.W. de Klerk, 36

failed state, 17

Ferdinand Lassalle, 3, 118

Ferdinand Marcos, 82

fiat money, 186

financial boogeyman, 104

Financial Times, 106

fluctuation of labor recompense, 193

Françafrique, 84

France, 33, 51, 66, 69, 71, 94, 103, 108, 177, 219

Fred Moseley, 5, 109

free market, 20, 198

Free Trade Zones, 62

Freemasonry, 187, 217

G

Gangnam, i, 39, 40, 43, 55, 131, 213

Garden of Eden, 186

Gaspar Yanga, 104

General Suharto, 37

General Than Shwe, 29, 216

genocide, 54

George Riesman, 122

Germain Garnier, 114

Germany, 19, 45, 177, 189

Gerold Lauck, 138

global economic system, 21

global financial transactions, 20

globalization, 16, 61, 63

Graham Bell, 175

Greece, 45, 75, 114, 131

greed, 38, 45, 53, 62, 73, 82, 106, 109, 120, 188, 189

Gridley Bryant, 185

Gross Domestic Product, 7, 16,
    25, 93, 214, 215
growth, 7, 19, 45, 60, 74, 81, 96,
    98, 114, 117, 156, 193
Guatemala, 75, 177
guillotine, 50, 67, 136, 143
Gyanendra Shah, 72

H

Haiti, iii, 17, 101, 102, 103, 104,
    214
Harry Dexter White, 18
Harry Gordon Selfridge, 139
hedonism, 131
Henri Poincaré, 175
heterox, 1, 109, 204
Heterox economics, 1
Hillary Rodham Clinton, 152
Hiram Abiff, 187
homeless, 26, 29, 107
hookworms, 81
Horace A.W. Tabor, 178
humiliation, 29, 37, 93, 95
hurricane Katrina, 32

I

ideas, viii, 5, 120, 123, 175, 200,
    201
ideologues, 184
ignore, i, ii, 25, 32, 108, 110, 125,
    132, 158, 172

IMF, 16, 80, 214
imposition, 16, 156
India, 7, 27, 28, 57, 58, 75, 95, 96,
    97, 99, 177, 191, 214, 215,
    216
Indian space program's (I.S.R.O),
    27
indifference, 42, 107, 146, 151,
    152, 153, 172, 195, 198
indignation, 22, 95, 132
individual means, 191, 199
inequality, iii, 6, 62, 66, 74, 125,
    130, 179, 204
information, 49, 61, 91, 153, 161,
    172
inhumane conditions, 60
institutionalism, 1
intellectual "Waterloo", 13
intellectual freedom, 196
intellectual midgets, 83
intensity, 10, 75
interest, 100, 106, 111, 114, 117,
    118, 120, 121, 122, 142, 146,
    150, 204
international financial
    institutions, 16, 18
International Monetary Fund,
    16, 17
Internet, 202
involvement, 192, 196, 199, 201
Iran, 84, 93
Ireland, 178

Isaak Illich Rubin, 119

Israel, 99, 100

Istvan Romer, 174

Ivar Kreuger, 176

J

Jacob Astor, 53, 217

James Tobin, 9

Janos Irinyi, 174

Japan, 180

Jean-Baptiste Say, 105, 132

Jean-Bédel Bokassa, 71

Jefferson Davis, 178

Jesse Livermore, 73

John Davison, 113

John Harvey Kellogg, 123, 218

John Pilger, 37

José de la Cruz Porfirio Díaz
    Mori, 156

Joseph Goebbels, 68

just price, 158, 200

K

kamikaze, 22

Karl Marx, 3, 66, 110, 118, 137,
    159, 184, 185, 197

Kenya, ii, 4, 6, 79, 177

Keynes, 18, 78, 79, 105, 184

Keynesian, 72

Khap Panchayats, 57

Kibera, ii, 220

King Juan Carlos of Spain, 70

King Leopold II, 19, 54, 172

King Mswati III, 70

L

laborers, 15, 49, 50, 63, 67, 109,
    112, 115, 117, 118, 122, 145,
    159, 171, 181, 187, 190, 191,
    192, 195, 199, 200, 201

laboring class, 109, 115, 122, 133,
    184, 189

lack of bon sens and no sense of
    urgency melting pot, 103

laissez faire utopia, 114

lampooning, 21, 184

landowners, 108, 109, 112, 189,
    190, 191, 192, 199, 200

leadership, 16, 30, 154, 156

Libya, 92, 191

Lilith, 99, 186

Louis Blanc, 119

Lucifer, 88, 99

Lula da Silva, 96

lumpenintellectuals, 160

lumpenintelligentsias, 185

M

M. Night Shyamalan, 23

madrassas, 203

make, sell, and buy, 195, 205

Malthus, 51, 121

Mama Vincent, i, 6, 130

Mandela, 35, 36, 37, 38, 39

Mansa Abu Bakr, 172

Mao Zedong, 95

Maori, 45

marginalized, 19

Marikana massacre, 39

market clearing, 193

Marxian, 72

Marxist, 3, 5

Maximillian Robespierre, 100

metamorphosis, 93

Mexican revolution, 156

Mexico, 84, 91, 156, 177

Michael Bloomberg, 25

Michał Kalecki, 184, 185

Michele Obama, 46

Mikhail Gorbachev, 96

military junta, 30

Milton Friedman, viii

minimum wage, 22, 61, 63, 125,
    170, 180, 190

mismanagement, 14, 18

Mobutu Sese Seko, 83

Mohamed Bouazizi, i, 89, 95, 132

Mohammed Bouazizi, 104

monarchy, 69, 70, 71

Monarchy, 72

Monetarists, 72

money, 13, 26, 32, 33, 38, 41, 40,
    46, 62, 68, 69, 72, 74, 80, 84,
    85, 98, 106, 113, 121, 122,
    131, 136, 137, 155, 157, 158,
    168, 173, 177

moneyers, 159, 168, 179, 188,
    189, 190, 191, 192, 193, 199,
    200, 204

Monica Lewinski, 46

Monsanto, 97

Moriori, 45

Muammar al-Gaddafi, 92

Muammar Gaddafi, 191

Mukesh Ambani, 28, 62, 216

Mumbai, 27, 28, 214

N

Namibia, 136, 216

Nancy Reagan, 46

Napoleon Bonaparte, 64, 65

Napoleonic Wars, 108

Narasimha Rao, 96

narco corridor, 91

NASDAQ, 25

Nassau Senior, viii, 109, 110,
    111, 115, 116, 119, 126, 133,
    145, 185, 188, 213, 215

Nassau William Senior
    abstinence theory, 62

Native Americans, 53

necessaries, 146

necessities, 118, 145, 173

Nelson Mandela, 1

Nepial, 72

New classical, 72

new mindset, 186

New Orleans, 30, 31, 32, 33, 169, 215, 219

New Thinking and Old books, 131

New York City, 24, 25, 26, 31, 40, 41, 75

New York Stock Exchange, 25

New Zealand, 45, 177

Nicholas Sarkozy, 92

Niger, 51, 185, 217

Niger Delta boys, 65

Nigeria, 14, 60, 65, 84, 125, 177, 217

Nikola Tesla, 175

Niyamgiri hill, 57

Noah's Ark, 35, 36

non-profit based enterprises, 200

Ntamugenga, 174

O

obsession, 24, 44, 45, 47, 98, 202

Occupy Wall Street, 7

ordinance, 6

Oriel Noetic, 112, 113

orthodox, 109, 204

overconsumption, 47, 48, 205

P

P. Chidambaram, 27

Pakistan, 49, 177, 198

Palestine, 99, 188

panhandling, ii, 40, 41

paradox, 42

participation, 192, 196, 198, 199, 200, 201

passion, 10, 15, 94

patent and start-up fund trap, 175, 199

Patrice Motsepe, 68

Paul Biya, 71

Paul Krugman, 131

percentage of the surplus, 199

Peter Eigen, 80

Philippines, 82, 177

Philo Taylor Farnsworth, 174

Piero Sraffa, 159

political economy, 110, 112, 113, 116, 156, 167, 169

pollution, 21

Ponzi scheme, 176

Poor Law Inquiry Commission, 113

poor people, i, 23, 24, 32, 42, 66, 130, 159

Pope Francis, 107, 125

potency, 7

poverty, ii, iii, 6, 20, 21, 23, 30, 34, 35, 38, 40, 42, 46, 51, 60, 81, 95, 102, 107, 112, 119, 130, 178

predatory skills, 125

preference, 74, 102, 118, 121, 150, 151

profit, 50, 107, 108, 157, 158, 195, 199, 200, 201, 202

Profit led enterprises, 200

profiteers, 115, 133, 167, 171,
    176, 180, 184, 185, 189, 197,
    204

propensity of action, 146

Proximity value, 145

Psy, 39, 40

psychiatric Capitalism facility,
    21

puppeteers, 46

Q

quantum paradigm, 205

R

rationale, 110

Ray Nagin, 32

recompense, 115, 155, 171, 180,
    191, 192, 195, 199, 201

Red Obsession, 141

rejuvenate, 21

relevance, 1, 7, 69

Religion, 64, 68, 69

repression, 14, 30, 116, 168

Republic of the Congo, 79

resilience, iii, 49

resistance, 74, 143

resource waste, 18

responsibility, i, 8, 36, 145, 152,
    168

rethinking economics, 205

revenue, 69, 199, 200, 201, 202

Revenue led enterprises, 200

reverend Graham, 123

Ricardo, 78, 108, 110, 114, 121,
    137, 156, 158, 159, 160, 218

Richard Whately, 112

Riggs Bank, 33

risk premium, 121

Robert Reich, 60, 61, 63

Rod Blagojevich, 14

Russia, 7, 75, 93, 95, 98, 99, 214

Russian oligarchy, 7

Rwanda, 4, 99

S

Saddam Hussein, 83, 84

Salvador Allende, 104

Sarah Baartman Hottentot
    Venus., 43

Saudi Arabia, 25, 177

Schumpeter, 161, 192

Sean Quinn, 178

self-annihilation, 47

self-enslavement, 16, 156, 173,
    188

Senior's Abstinence theory, 110,
    115, 116, 117, 119, 120, 124

Sentimental value, 145

Sharpeville massacre, 39

shime-waza, 92

Siddhārtha Gautama, 172

Silicon Valley, 55, 58, 199

Sir Paul Collier, 67

skewedness, 8

slavery, 16, 22, 41, 47, 53, 79, 95,
    103, 106

slaves, 46, 103, 154, 172, 178

socialism, 96

Socialism, 8, 197

society, ii, 4, 13, 16, 27, 36, 39,
    40, 42, 40, 48, 71, 73, 92, 123,
    140, 181

socio-economic inequality, 2, 10,
    68

South Africa, 2, 36, 37, 95, 99,
    177, 213, 220

South Korea, 40, 45, 177, 216

Spain, 45, 177

Statute of Jewry, 106

Steve Biko, 104

stubbornness, 96

Sudan, 84

supremacy of Capitalism, 196

surplus, 160, 191, 192, 200, 201,
    204

sustainable solution, 21

Sustenance value, 145

Swami Vivekananda, 10

Swaziland, 35, 70, 219

Switzerland, 25, 177

T

Tāufaʻāhau Tupou IV, 72

Teodoro Nguema Obiang, 33, 34,
    35

Thailand, 153, 177

The Great Depression, 74, 217

The Wealth of Nations, 167, 170,
    171, 184, 219

third world countries, 15, 19, 32,
    41, 48, 68, 80, 81

Thomas Edison, 175

Thomas Hodgskin, 159

Thomas Piketty, 10, 106, 179

Thomas Robert Malthus, 51, 105

Thorstein Veblen, 131, 146

tiptoeing, 9, 160

Togo, 94, 153

Tony Blair, 92, 155

tour du poor monde, 15

Toussaint Louverture, 101

Trinidad and Tobago, 41

Tver City, iii

U

Uganda, 41, 198

unemployment, 65, 133, 154, 181,
    192

Union of Myanmar, 29

United Kingdom, 27, 110, 113,
    119, 155, 168, 177

United Nations, 4, 18, 25

United States, iii, vii, 4, 14, 20,
    24, 26, 27, 30, 32, 33, 40, 39,
    42, 46, 49, 58, 61, 63, 64, 82,
    89, 90, 91, 97, 99, 109, 123,

143, 152, 154, 155, 169, 176,
177, 186

universal living recompense, iv

uranium, 51

US veterans, 26

V

Vedanta, 57, 59, 60, 215

Viktor Yanukovych, 132

Vladimir Vladimirovich Putin, 7,
153

Vladimir Zworykin, 174

voodoo, 17, 41, 102, 103, 153

W

Wales, 60

Walmart, 50, 141, 180

Walter Shaw, 199

war, 6, 21, 46, 96, 108, 119, 141,
155, 178

wealth accumulation, 62, 176,
179, 180, 185

wealth distribution, 110, 193, 195

Western revisionists, 19

William Godwin, 11

World Bank, 16, 17, 27, 80, 81

Z

Zacharies Lewala, 136

Special Thanks

To special people across the globe

Canada Toronto - The woman at the airport - for helping me retrieve my laptop

DRC Goma - Christine Musaidizi- for the revealing dialogue

Ethiopia Addis Ababa - Genet Kefetew & "Paulos" - for the late evening meals & stimulating debate

Haiti Milot - Couronne - for showing us the top of the world
Australia - Donald Kayembe Henry - for losing your mind

Jordan- Mohammad Al-Zou'bi – for his humility

Nigeria - Honorable Aminu Abbas - for the matchstick

Russia Moscow - Maxim Akhmetvaliev - for your support

Senegal Dakar - Kalle Mbuyi - for your enthusiasm

UK London – Angie - for the great work

US Florida - Guy Brisson Vastey – for the roar and addiction

US Florida - Mihalis Halkides - for your madness

US Florida – Narcisse Meillon- for your responsive contribution

US Florida – Samantha L. Shakur Bowden - for the question

US Florida - Darius Wynn - for his relentless positivity

US Florida - Vivian Jones - for her non-conventional support

US Massachusetts – Jonathan Donald Jenner – for the paranoia

US Massachusetts – Natalie Williams- for the nuggets

US Texas - Kouka Matingou Christian Elvis - for the wakeup call

US Massachusetts-Jessica Davin-Staples- for the password

To my team of mothers who have kept me grounded:

Mama Jules Nzunzu, Mama Gitari, Mama Pitchou Matundu, Mama Otoko, and Mama Medard.

To people who have kept me alive:

Dr Omanga, Dr Mashako, Dr Serushago, Dr Mizerero, Nurse Mafama, and above all, to my grandmother Sofia, whose deep ancestral knowledge of medicine cured my asthma.

And finally

Throughout this journey, if I did not touch on your country, city or cited your name, my hope is that in my examples, you were able to somehow relate to the faces and narratives I've described.

R.I.P Sekimonyo Mugemanyi Mathias (my gracious grandfather) and Nteguye Murekatete Sophie (my jovial grandmother)

CPSIA information can be obtained at www.ICGtesting.com
Printed in the USA
BVOW01s2040081114

374108BV00002B/5/P